THE DIABETIC
COOKBOOK

THE DIABETIC COOKBOOK

BRIDGET JONES

APPLE

A QUINTET BOOK

Published by The Apple Press
6 Blundell Street
London N7 9BH

Reprinted in 1995, 1997

ISBN 1-85076-480-8

This book was designed and produced by
Quintet Publishing Limited
6 Blundell Street
London N7 9BH

Creative Director: Richard Dewing
Designer: Stuart Walden
Project Editor: Damian Thompson
Editor: Joy Wotton
Photographer: Trevor Wood
Nutritional analyst: Jane Griffin

Typeset in Great Britain by
Central Southern Typesetters, Eastbourne
Manufactured in Hong Kong by
Regent Publishing Services Limited
Printed in Singapore by
Star Standard Industries private Ltd

CONTENTS

BEFORE USING THE RECIPES

METRIC/IMPERIAL

All weights and measures are presented in both metric and imperial: follow only one set of measures as they are not interchangeable.

SPOON MEASURES

These are all standard British spoon measures – do not use serving cutlery or table cutlery. Buy a good set of modern measuring spoons which have deep bowls so that dry ingredients may be levelled off easily with a knife. All spoon measures are level unless otherwise stated.

SWEETENER

A granular sweetener has been used for testing; that is, a sweetener suitable for sprinkling over food. In the baking recipes a sweetener recommended for cooking was selected; however, since these products contain saccharine they tend to leave a bitter aftertaste which can be unpleasant in lighter cooking. Therefore for all other purposes an aspartame-based sweetener has been used.

Note that aspartame sweeteners lose their sweetness during cooking but they are suitable for adding to hot foods, such as drinks or pickles and chutneys that have been removed from the heat. Aspartame is often sold under the NutraSweet brand.

Saccharine-based sweeteners, or sweeteners with a proportion of saccharine, react badly flavour-wise with certain ingredients – particularly tangy low-fat soft cheese and cocoa.

Please note the information on the sweetener label for details of its carbohydrate content.

KEEPING QUALITY OF UNSWEETENED BAKING AND PRESERVES

Cakes and other baked items that rely on their sugar content for good keeping qualities will not keep well when made without sugar. In normal storage conditions they become mouldy and inedible in 2–3 days, depending on the dried fruit content. Storing these foods in the refrigerator (in an airtight polythene bag) helps but it is better to cook frequently and in small batches or to freeze baked items.

In the case of pickles, the vinegar content acts as a preservative; however the keeping quality may not be as good as when sugar is also included. Store pickles in a cool, dry, dark place and keep them in the refrigerator once opened. The recipes tested for the pickles in this book have all been stored successfully in a cool room for 2 months. They should keep well for at least 3 months, probably up to 6 months; however, it pays to be aware of their possible shortfalls and to look for any signs of deterioration in quality.

FOOD VALUES

Each recipe is headed with a box containing food values for the completed dish. This information provides a carbohydrate value, which is important if you have to count the total carbohydrate in your daily diet. The amount of fibre, fat and kilocalories/joules is a useful guide to balanced eating when they are considered in the context of your overall daily or weekly diet. The values are given as a total for the whole recipe or per portion for the recommended number of servings. If the number of servings is reduced or increased, the values should be adjusted accordingly.

BELOW This diagram shows different kinds of food, and the proportions in which they are beneficial to the diabetic's diet.

RULES TO REMEMBER

■ Follow your doctor's, dietitian's or clinic's advice on diet and life style and consult them with all queries and problems.

■ Be sure to attend for regular health checks and never change your diet or eating patterns without consulting your doctor, dietitian or clinic beforehand.

■ Eat regular meals and snacks throughout the day. Your calorie intake should fit your requirements so that you do not gain or lose weight except under medical supervision.

■ Do not miss or avoid meals and carry suitable snacks when travelling or staying away from home.

■ Remember that when you are more active you use up more carbohydrate. If you have a day when you expend far less energy than usual, then your body will use less carbohydrate.

■ If you have to count carbohydrates, then make it second nature to check labels. Be aware of what you are eating. Buy an authoritative booklet which lists food values.

■ Maintain a balanced diet by eating a broad variety of foods on a regular basis.

■ Decrease or cut out sugar and sweetened foods according to your doctor's advice.

■ Avoid sweetened manufactured foods which do not have a clear indication of their sugar content on the label.

■ Increase your intake of high-fibre foods, if necessary, to moderate the rate of sugar absorption in your body as well as for general good health.

■ Moderate or lower your intake of fats, if necessary. Balance the fat content of your diet by eating more fat from vegetable sources than from animal products.

■ Eat plenty of fresh vegetables and fruit with a low sugar content.

■ Keep alcohol consumption to a minimum.

■ Keep yourself fit, healthy and active. Take regular exercise, according to your doctor's advice.

FOREWORD

If you are recently diagnosed as having diabetes, you are probably just beginning to adapt to a new way of eating and you may well be more aware of the dietary restrictions than of the positive side of the nutrition advice you have been given. The most important point to appreciate is that your diet does not have to be "different" or odd and it certainly does not have to impose social restrictions – in fact, the general advice about good eating is in tune with the recommendations made to the population as a whole.

This book presents a wide variety of recipes specially written to fit in with the guidelines given to those following a diabetic diet. It is not a "diet" book and I am not a doctor nor a dietitian. The theory of balanced eating and avoiding the significant use of pure sugar is translated into practical cooking for every occasion.

Bon appetit!

BREAKFASTS

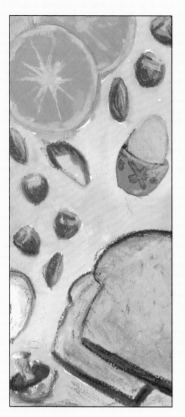

Eating a sensible breakfast is important to provide an adequate supply of carbohydrate for the morning's activity. A high-fibre, low-sugar meal is ideal. As many commercial breakfast cereals have a high sugar content, I have included a few alternative suggestions in this chapter.

It is best to avoid eating a traditional fried breakfast on a regular basis, saving it for an occasional treat, and then opting for grilled bacon and poached or scrambled eggs. Eggs, mushrooms and tomatoes are all excellent served on wholemeal toast. Baked beans are a satisfying snack or breakfast food but look for brands which do not have added sugar.

The citrus spreads and fruit spreads in the final chapter are perfect replacements for high-sugar traditional marmalades.

Fresh fruit and fruit salads are versatile for breakfast or a snack, particularly citrus fruits, strawberries, watermelon and soft fruits that have a low sugar content. Try stewed rhubarb or gooseberries with a non-sugar sweetener for a change – they are good cold, topped with natural yoghurt.

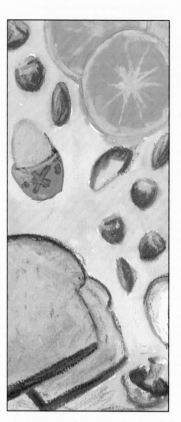

HOME-MADE MUESLI

MAKES ABOUT **300G/9OZ**

Many wholefood shops sell bags of mixed grains ready for making muesli. Otherwise keep the mixture as plain or as varied as you like – a simple combination of porridge oats (an excellent source of soluble fibre) and fruit is perfectly good.

FOOD VALUES	CARBOHYDRATE	FIBRE	FAT	KCALS/KJ
TOTAL	291G	65G	83G	2026/8534
PER PORTION	(65G/2½OZ) 36G	8G	10G	253/1067

(Above values do not include milk or yoghurt)

- *100 g/4 oz rolled oats* ● *50 g/2 oz bran* ● *50 g/2 oz wheat or millet flakes*
75 g/3 oz raisins ● *75 g/3 oz sultanas*
● *50 g/2 oz dried apple rings, chopped*
● *100 g/4 oz ready-to-eat dried apricots, chopped*
● *100 g/4 oz walnuts, chopped*

1 Mix all the ingredients in a large bowl, then store the museli in an airtight container in a cool, dry cupboard.

2 Serve with milk (skimmed or semi-skimmed) or natural yoghurt. Fresh fruit, such as banana, grapes or peach, may be served with the muesli. For a special breakfast, combine a selection of chopped fresh fruits with the muesli but remember to add their carbohydrate values to that of the cereal mixture.

GRAPEFRUIT COCKTAILS

SERVES **4**

As for other citrus fruit, grapefruit is believed to slow down the rate of sugar metabolism. Here the fruit is transformed into three lively cocktails to start the day or begin a meal.

FOOD VALUES	CARBOHYDRATE	FIBRE	FAT	KCALS/KJ
GRAPE COCKTAIL PER PORTION	16.4G	2.6G	0.4G	70/300
MELON COCKTAIL PER PORTION	19.3G	2.5G	0.5G	83/356
BANANA AND ORANGE COCKTAIL PER PORTION	28.6G	4.3G	3.9G	158/669

- *2 large juicy grapefruit*

1 Peel the grapefruit and remove all the pith. Hold the fruit over a basin and use a sharp serrated knife to cut in towards the middle of the fruit, removing the fleshy segments and leaving behind the membranes that separate them. Catch all the juice. This is the foundation for the three cocktails below.

GRAPE COCKTAIL

- *100 g/4 oz seedless green grapes* • *2 kiwi fruit, peeled, halved and sliced*
- *4 mint sprigs*

1 Leave small grapes whole or halve larger ones and mix them with the grapefruit. Add the kiwi fruit and mint, then mix lightly.

MELON COCKTAIL

- *5-cm/2-in piece fresh root ginger, peeled and chopped*
- *a little water* • *1 tbsp sweetener* • *1 tbsp rose-water*
- *¼ honeydew melon* • *large wedge watermelon*

1 Place the ginger in a small saucepan with water to cover. Bring to the boil, cover and simmer for 30 minutes, making sure the water does not evaporate. At the end of cooking boil the ginger, if necessary, until the liquid is reduced to 2 tbsp or slightly less. Leave to cool, then stir in the sweetener and rose-water.

2 Discard the seeds and peel from both types of melon, then cut them into small neat cubes. Mix the melon with the grapefruit and strain the ginger juice over. Chill for at least 30 minutes before serving.

BANANA AND ORANGE COCKTAIL

- *2 oranges* • *2 bananas* • *2 tbsp flaked almonds, toasted*

1 Remove the orange segments as for the grapefruit, then mix both citrus segments. (These may be covered and chilled ahead of time or overnight.) Just before serving, slice the bananas and mix them into the fruit. Spoon into dishes and top with almonds, then serve at once.

RAISIN BRAN CRUNCH

MAKES ABOUT **950G/2LB 3OZ**

FOOD VALUES	CARBOHYDRATE	FIBRE	FAT	KCALS/KJ
TOTAL	314G	111G	189G	3008/12604
PER PORTION	(100G/4OZ) 39G	14G	24G	376/1576

(Above values do not include milk or yoghurt)

- *175 g/6 oz raisins* ● *225 g/8 oz bran* ● *100 g/4 oz rolled oats*
  - *12 tbsp sesame seeds (preferably unroasted)*
    - *10 tbsp sunflower seeds (unroasted)*
    - *450 ml/³/₄ pt unsweetened orange juice*

1 Mix the raisins, bran, oats and both types of seeds in a large bowl, then stir in the orange juice.

2 Set the oven at 160°C, 325°F, gas 3.

3 Lightly grease a large roasting tin. Stir the mixture thoroughly, then turn it into the tin – do not press it down. Bake for about 2 hours, turning and stirring occasionally, until well-browned, crisp and dry.

4 Allow to cool in the tin, then break the mixture up into small lumps and store them in an airtight container.

5 Serve with milk.

APPLE BULGUR BREAKFAST

SERVES **8**

This may sound very strange but, if you like bulgur and yoghurt, it makes a pleasing, satisfying breakfast dish or snack. My original intention when testing was to add oats to the soaked bulgur, then bake it until it formed a crisp cereal to eat with milk. I had to have a quick taste after soaking the grain and it tasted so good that I decided to leave well alone – it made a great mid-morning snack in the middle of testing recipes! Vary the fruit, if you like, or add fresh fruit to the plain soaked bulgur.

FOOD VALUES	CARBOHYDRATE	FIBRE	FAT	KCALS/KJ
TOTAL	64G	3G	4G	352/1486
PER PORTION	8G	0.5G	0.5G	44/186

- *25 g/1 oz dried apple rings, chopped* ● *40 g/1¹/₂ oz bulgur*
  - *150 ml/¹/₄ pt natural yoghurt or fromage frais*
    - *50 ml/2 fl oz milk* ● *a little sweetener (optional)*

1 Mix the apple and bulgur in a basin, then stir in the yoghurt or fromage frais and half the milk. Cover and set aside for 30 minutes, or until the bulgur is softened and swollen.

2 The grain should still have some bite, although it can be left covered in the refrigerator overnight. Stir well and add extra milk as necessary to make the mixture creamy. The mixture can be sweetened with sweetener if liked.

FIRST COURSES

This is a chapter of light dishes that are ideal for starting any special meal. Serve them with wholemeal bread, rolls or toast to begin the meal on a well-balanced basis.

You may prefer to opt for an opening course more regularly instead of making a dessert. If so, use the lower fat and high-fibre ingredients but on special occasions feel free to indulge the taste-buds with creamy concoctions.

In addition to the recipes here, remember that fruit cocktails make refreshing starters or serve one or more colourful vegetable salads. A topping of chopped nuts, crunchy bread croûtons or very crisp grilled bacon, crumbled into small pieces, adds texture and considerable flavour.

If you are looking for ideas for a light lunch, then simply increase the quantities to make the portions more substantial and serve with baked potatoes.

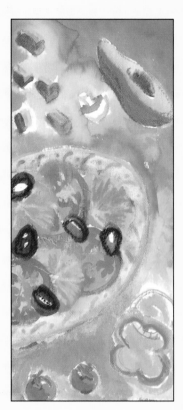

CREAMY GARLIC MUSHROOMS

SERVES **4**

These are perfect baked-potato fillers!

FOOD VALUES	CARBOHYDRATE	FIBRE	FAT	KCALS/KJ
TOTAL	8G	12.5G	49G	566 /2345
PER PORTION	2G	3G	12G	142/586

- *2 tbsp olive oil* ● *1 large garlic clove, crushed*
- *2 spring onions, chopped* ● *salt and freshly ground black pepper*
- *350 g/12 oz button mushrooms* ● *175 g/6 oz low-fat soft cheese*
- *a little parsley, chopped (optional)*

1 Heat the oil in a large frying-pan. Add the garlic, onions and seasoning, and cook for 2 minutes. Then add all the mushrooms and toss them over high heat for a couple of minutes, until they are hot. Do not cook the mushrooms until their juices run as they will be too watery.

2 Make a clearing in the middle of the mushrooms, add the soft cheese and stir it for a few seconds, until it begins to soften. Gradually mix all the mushrooms with the cheese until they are evenly coated.

3 Divide between individual plates or dishes and top with a little chopped parsley if liked. Serve at once with warmed granary bread or toast.

4 Alternatively, transfer the mushrooms to a bowl, cool, then cover and chill them briefly before serving.

LETTUCE CUPS

SERVES 4

FOOD VALUES	CARBOHYDRATE	FIBRE	FAT	KCALS/KJ
TOTAL	55.5G	8G	76G	897/3735
PER PORTION	14G	2G	19G	224/934

- 50 g/2 oz long-grain brown rice ● salt and freshly ground black pepper
- grated rind of ½ lemon ● 250 ml/8 fl oz water ● 4 tbsp walnuts, chopped
- 1 tbsp fresh mint, chopped ● 2 tbsp parsley, chopped
- 1 tbsp olive oil ● a little lemon juice ● 4 iceberg or cos lettuce leaves
- 4 tomatoes, peeled, if liked, and diced ● 2 spring onions, chopped

1 Place the rice in a small saucepan with a sprinkling of salt and the lemon rind. Pour in the water and bring to the boil. Stir once, reduce the heat and cover the pan. Cook the rice gently for 25 minutes, or until only just tender. Leave the lid on the pan, removed from the heat, for 5 minutes by which time the rice should be tender and dry.

2 Add the walnuts, mint, parsley, oil and lemon juice to the hot rice, then fork the ingredients into the grains until well mixed. Cover and leave to cool.

3 Place a lettuce leaf on each serving plate. Divide the rice mixture between the lettuce cups, spooning it into a ring shape on each. Mix the tomatoes and spring onions and pile the mixture in the middle of the rice rings.

4 Serve with French dressing, if liked, and warm crusty bread.

COOK'S TIP
PEELING TOMATOES (AND PEACHES)

There are two methods: the first option is to spear a tomato on a metal fork, then hold it over a gas-burner until the skin blisters and bursts. Douse the tomato in cold water and rub off the skin. This method is fine for 1–4 tomatoes (assuming, of course, that you have a gas hob!).

For a large number, place the tomatoes in a bowl or basin and pour freshly boiling water from the kettle over them to cover them completely. Leave to stand for 30–60 seconds: the riper the fruit the quicker the skins loosen (under-ripe fruit may take up to 1½ minutes). If the tomatoes are left for too long, they begin to cook and soften. Drain them in a colander and use a pointed knife to slit the skins which will slide off easily. This method of blanching the fruit may also be used to peel peaches, leaving them to stand for about 2 minutes, again depending on ripeness.

COURGETTE-STUFFED MUSHROOMS

SERVES 4

FOOD VALUES	CARBOHYDRATE	FIBRE	FAT	KCALS/KJ
TOTAL	4G	3G	42.5G	618/2570
PER PORTION	1G	0.5G	11G	154/642

- 4 large open mushrooms • 2 courgettes (about 225 g/8 oz in weight,
- salt and freshly ground black pepper
- a little fresh lemon juice • 1 tsp dried oregano
- 2 tbsp grated Parmesan cheese
- 150 g/5 oz mozzarella cheese, sliced

1 Set the oven at 200°C, 400°F, gas 6.

2 Rinse the tops of the mushrooms, avoiding wetting the stalk side, wipe with absorbent kitchen paper and cut off the stalks. Place the mushroom caps on a baking dish or in a roasting tin.

3 Chop the stalks from the mushrooms and place them in a bowl. Trim, thinly peel and coarsely grate the courgettes. Drain them in a sieve, squeezing well to remove excess moisture, then mix them with the chopped stalks. Toss in the seasoning, lemon juice, oregano and Parmesan.

4 Divide the courgette mixture between the mushrooms and top each with a slice of mozzarella. Bake for about 20 minutes, or until the cheese is melted and browned.

5 Serve at once, with warm crusty bread to mop up the juices.

SERVING SUGGESTION

Toast four slices of granary bread and use a large round cutter or saucer to cut out circles of toast from the bread. Put these on the plates, then place a mushroom on each one – the toast absorbs the juices as the mushroom is cut and provides a crunchy contrast in texture. Fresh herb sprigs, such as parsley or basil may be added as a garnish, if wished.

SMOKED MACKEREL PÂTÉ

SERVES 4

FOOD VALUES	CARBOHYDRATE	FIBRE	FAT	KCALS/KJ
TOTAL	9G	0.5G	157.5G	1838/7613
PER PORTION	2G	0.1G	39G	460/1903

- 2 large smoked mackerel fillets ● 1 thin slice onion, finely chopped
- grated rind and juice of ½ lemon
- 225 g/8 oz soft cheese (use a smooth low-fat cheese, such as curd cheese, quark or cream cheese; cottage cheese is not suitable)
- 2 tbsp finely chopped parsley ● salt and freshly ground black pepper
- black olives to serve ● lemon wedges to serve

1 Flake all the mackerel off the skin, discarding the bones as you do so. Mix the mackerel with the onion and lemon rind, then work in the soft cheese until thoroughly combined.

2 Add lemon juice and seasoning to taste. Spoon the pâté into one dish or four individual dishes. Fork the top neatly, cover and chill briefly before serving with black olives and thick lemon wedges (for their juice), and melba toast, granary toast or warmed crusty bread.

VARIATIONS
SMOKED SALMON OR TROUT PÂTÉ

Use 175 g/6 oz smoked salmon or trout fillet instead of the mackerel. Pound the fillet to a paste or process it in a food processor or liquidizer. Continue as above.

SARDINE OR TUNA PÂTÉ

Substitute a drained 198 g/7 oz can tuna in brine or oil, or sardines in oil for the smoked mackerel. A crushed clove of garlic may be added instead of the onion.

STUFFED TOMATOES

Use the pâté to fill 8 medium-sized tomatoes. Slice the tops off the tomatoes, chop them and add them to the pâté. Scoop out the pips and pulp from the middle of the tomatoes – this may be added to the pâté or reserved for another use.

PÂTÉ IN LEMON SHELLS

This looks good for dinner-party starters but it is wasteful unless you particularly want to use the lemon flesh for making lemonade or some other dish. Cut the tops off four lemons, and cut a fine sliver off the base of each so they stand neatly. Use the point of a knife to begin to free the flesh from inside the shells, then use a teaspoon to scoop them out clean. Fill with pâté and replace the lids at an angle. Serve on a bed of lettuce.

LIGHT HUMMUS

SERVES 4

FOOD VALUES	CARBOHYDRATE	FIBRE	FAT	KCALS/KJ
TOTAL	78G	18G	35G	789/3315
PER PORTION	19.5G	4.5G	9G	197/829

(Above values do not include pitta bread or crusty bread)

- 125 g/15 oz can chick-peas, drained ● 1 garlic clove, crushed
- ½ small onion, very finely chopped or grated
- 150 g/5 oz firm-textured low-fat soft cheese (such as Shape or light Philadelphia cheese) ● about 2 tbsp milk
- salt and freshly ground black pepper

1 Thoroughly mash the chick-peas or purée them in a food processor or liquidizer. Mix in the garlic and onion, then gradually beat in the soft cheese and continue beating until the cheese and chick-peas are well combined.

2 Mix in enough milk to soften the hummus slightly and add seasoning to taste. Transfer the hummus to a serving dish, cover it and leave to chill for 30 minutes before serving.

3 Offer warm pitta bread or crusty bread with the hummus.

FISH AND SEAFOOD

Fish and seafood are excellent foods to include in every balanced diet, since they are low in fat and there is some indication that the fat content of oily fish may be beneficial.

Buy from a reputable fishmonger and you can expect virtually all the preparation to be carried out for you – with a smile and without any additional charge. Use fresh fish within a day of purchase.

The majority of frozen fish is excellent quality, it thaws quickly and is a useful stand-by for last-minute cooking since it can be cooked from frozen (although it does benefit from thawing first in a cool room or the refrigerator). If you are buying fish for freezing, make sure it is absolutely fresh – the eyes should be bright and the flesh firm and free of slime – and that it has not been frozen and thawed prior to sale.

TUNA BURGERS

SERVES 4

These are scrummy! Children seem to favour canned tuna above other fish (with the exception of fish fingers) and this is a popular way of introducing fish to their diet. Other canned fish may be used: salmon transforms the burgers into a special treat (or shape eight small patties to serve as a dinner-party starter with some tartare sauce); sardines in tomato sauce, kippers or mackerel all give good results.

FOOD VALUES	CARBOHYDRATE	FIBRE	FAT	KCALS/KJ
TOTAL	146G	11G	18G	988/4188
PER PORTION	37G	3G	4G	247/1047

- 198 g/7 oz can tuna in brine, drained ● 1 large onion, finely chopped
- 100 g/4 oz fresh wholemeal breadcrumbs
- salt and freshly ground black pepper ● 75 ml/3 fl oz milk
- 4 tbsp plain flour for coating ● 1 tbsp oil for brushing

1 Thoroughly mash the tuna, then mix in the onion and breadcrumbs. Add seasoning and mix well before stirring in enough milk to bind the mixture.

2 Pat the mixture together in the bowl, then cut it into four portions. Sprinkle the flour on a clean surface and shape each portion of mixture into a burger measuring 7.5–10 cm/3–4 in in diameter. Coat the burgers well with flour when shaped.

3 Place the burgers under the grill for about 2 minutes before brushing lightly with oil – this short cooking firms the top of the burgers, making it easier to brush the oil on – then continue cooking for another 5 minutes, until crisp and well browned on top. Turn the burgers and cook as for the first side.

SERVING SUGGESTIONS

- Serve the burgers in toasted split buns, with lettuce, tomatoes and cucumber.
- Serve with baked beans and a baked potato.
- Make eight small burgers and serve them in pairs as a first course, with some tartare sauce or creamed horseradish and lemon wedges to garnish (for their juice).

SINGLE PORTION SUGGESTION

Use half a 100 g/4 oz can tuna, 2 chopped spring onions and 50 g/2 oz wholemeal breadcrumbs with 1–2 tbsp milk to make a single burger. Alternatively, make a delicious crab burger by using a 43 g/2 oz can dressed crab.

DIFFERENT FISH PIE

SERVES 4

This quick, and extremely tasty, fish dish is quite a departure from the traditional combination of fish in white sauce with mashed potato topping. Should you wish to make a traditional pie, the note at the end of the recipe outlines the quantities and method – but do try this first.

FOOD VALUES	CARBOHYDRATE	FIBRE	FAT	KCALS/KJ
TOTAL	192G	20G	49G	1944/8199
PER PORTION	48G	5G	12G	486/2050

- 1 kg/2¼ lb potatoes ● salt and freshly ground black pepper
- 675 g/1½ lb white fish fillet ● grated rind and juice of ½ lemon
- 2 tbsp oil (olive oil if you like the flavour) ● 1 onion, chopped
- 1 tsp dried marjoram or oregano ● 1 garlic clove, crushed (optional)
- 225 g/8 oz mushrooms, sliced ● 2 x 400 g/14 oz cans chopped tomatoes
- 2 tbsp chopped parsley ● 50 g/2 oz Cheddar cheese, grated

1 Cut the potatoes into thick slices, then into fingers (or chip shapes) and across into large dice. Place them in a large saucepan, add water to cover and a little salt. Put over medium heat, until the water is just boiling.

2 Meanwhile, lay the fish on a large plate or dish to go on top of the saucepan of potatoes. Sprinkle with a little seasoning, the lemon rind and juice. Cover the fish with a second plate, lid or foil and put it on top of the potatoes when they are boiling. Reduce the heat, if necessary, so that the water is just boiling and cook for about 10 minutes, or until the potato dice are tender. Remove the fish but leave it covered on the plate. Drain the potatoes well.

3 While the potatoes are cooking, heat the oil in a frying-pan or flameproof casserole. Add the onion, marjoram or oregano and garlic, if used, and cook gently for about 20 minutes, until the onion is soft and well cooked.

4 Add the mushrooms to the onion and fry them for about 5 minutes before pouring in the tomatoes. Stir well, add a little

seasoning, and bring to the boil. Reduce the heat and let the mixture simmer gently while you remove the skin and bones from the fish.

5 Pour the juices from the fish into the tomato mixture, then flake the flesh (it should not be well cooked yet) into fairly large chunks. Discard the skin and all bones, then lightly stir the fish into the tomato mixture. Simmer for 5 minutes, until the fish is cooked and hot. Taste for seasoning and stir in the parsley.

6 Turn the fish mixture into a dish to go under the grill. Top with the potatoes, then sprinkle with the cheese. Place under a moderately hot grill until the cheese has melted and the potato topping is crisp and golden. Serve at once.

VARIATIONS
SINGLE PORTION SUGGESTION

Dice and cook 1 large potato. Use a small onion and a small can of tomatoes, and cook them in a little saucepan, then add a frozen cod or haddock steak when the tomato-and-mushroom mixture is simmering. Cover and cook for about 20 minutes, or until the fish is cooked through. Carefully flake the fish into bite-sized chunks in the pan before transferring to a dish for topping and grilling.

QUICK AND CREAMY FISH PIE

Cook the potatoes and fish as in the main recipe. Instead of the tomato sauce, heat a knob of butter or margarine in a saucepan, then stir in 40 g/1½ oz plain flour and gradually pour in 600 ml/ 1 pt milk, stirring all the time. Bring to the boil, stirring, then add 100 g/4 oz frozen peas and bring back to the boil. Reduce the heat and simmer for 5 minutes. Add the mushrooms (if liked) with the fish and its cooking juices, and cook for a further 3 minutes. Stir in the parsley and seasoning to taste, then top and grill as in the main recipe.

BAKED FISH CAKE

SERVES **4**

This is far easier to prepare than individual fish cakes coated with egg and breadcrumbs, and baking is the more satisfactory cooking method diet-wise.

FOOD VALUES	CARBOHYDRATE	FIBRE	FAT	KCALS/KJ
TOTAL	190G	12G	49G	1573/6629
PER PORTION	47.5G	3G	12G	393/1657

- 675 g/1½ lb potatoes, peeled ● 450 g/1 lb white fish fillet
- salt and freshly ground white or black pepper
- 25 g/1 oz butter ● 4 tbsp milk ● grated rind of ½ lemon
- 2 tbsp chopped parsley ● 1 tsp anchovy essence (optional)
- 3 tbsp plain flour ● 2 tbsp oil

1 Cut the potatoes into chunks and place them in a saucepan with enough water to cover, adding a little salt if liked. Heat until just about to boil.

2 Meanwhile, lay the fish on a plate or dish to cover the saucepan and cover it with a second plate, lid or foil. Put the fish on the pan when the water is boiling, then reduce the heat so that the water does not froth over. Cook the potatoes until tender – 10–15 minutes if the chunks are fairly small.

3 Set the fish aside, without uncovering it. Drain and mash the potatoes, beating them well until smooth. Mix in the butter, milk, lemon rind, parsley and anchovy essence if used.

4 Set the oven at 200°C, 400°F, gas 6.

5 Grease a flan dish or baking tin Pour any cooking juices from the fish into the potato mixture. Flake the flesh off the skin, discarding all bones, and add it to the potatoes. Mix well, adding seasoning to taste.

6 Use a large spoon to place the fish mixture in a mound on the prepared dish or tin but do not flatten it until it is all mounded up. Flatten the top of the mixture slightly, then sprinkle it with a little of the flour. Use a palette knife and slice to flatten the mixture into a neat round, about 18 cm/7 in across. Pat the sides with the knife and the top with the slice so that the mixture is even and neatly shaped, keep sprinkling with the flour to coat the outside evenly.

7 Trickle the oil over the fish cake and bake it for about 30 minutes, until well browned. Cut into wedges to serve.

COOK'S TIP
FREEZING THE FISH CAKES

The fish cake freezes well – make a double quantity and shape half the mixture into a round cake on a baking tray lined with freezer film or lightly greased foil. Open freeze the uncooked cake, then pack it in a freezer bag. Cook the fish cake from frozen, allowing an extra 10 minutes' cooking time at 190°C, 375°F, gas 5, or until the fish cake is hot through.

ALMOND-STUFFED PLAICE

SERVES **4**

Lemon sole fillets are excellent instead of the plaice – they are less expensive than true sole, or Dover sole which is best cooked on the bone since it yields very small, uneconomic fillets.

FOOD VALUES	CARBOHYDRATE	FIBRE	FAT	KCALS/KJ
TOTAL	72G	10G	78G	1723/7233
PER PORTION	18G	3G	20G	431/1808

- *50 g/2 oz ground almonds* • *50 g/2 oz fresh wholemeal breadcrumbs*
- *1 tbsp chopped parsley* • *2 tbsp snipped chives*
- *salt and freshly ground black pepper* • *about 2 tbsp milk*
- *8 small plaice fillets, skinned* • *2 tbsp oil or 25 g/1 oz butter*
- *25 g/1 oz flaked almonds* • *1 small onion, finely chopped*
- *1 tbsp plain flour* • *250 ml/8 fl oz dry white wine, medium cider or fish stock*
- *4 tbsp fromage frais or half-fat single cream*

1 Mix the almonds, breadcrumbs, parsley, half the chives and seasoning, then stir in enough milk to bind the ingredients in a firm stuffing.

2 Lay one plaice fillet on a plate, skinned side up. Place a little of the stuffing at the head end, then roll up the fillet and secure it with a wooden cocktail stick. Repeat with the remaining fillets.

3 Heat the oil or melt the butter in a frying-pan with a lid or a flameproof casserole. Add the flaked almonds and cook over medium heat, stirring occasionally, until they are lightly browned. Use a slotted spoon to remove the nuts from the pan, draining them well, and place them on absorbent kitchen paper; set aside.

4 Add the onion to the fat remaining in the pan and cook for about 10 minutes, until softened. Stir in the flour, then gradually pour in the liquid, stirring all the time. Bring to the boil, then reduce the heat so that the sauce just simmers. At this point, add a little seasoning.

5 Arrange the fish rolls in the sauce, cover the pan and regulate the heat so that the sauce is simmering gently. Cook for about 20 minutes, or until the fish rolls are cooked through – do not over-cook the fish as it will lack flavour and texture.

6 Transfer the rolls to a heated serving dish or plates and remove the cocktail sticks. Stir the fromage frais or cream into the sauce and stir well. Taste for seasoning, then spoon the sauce over the fish rolls. Top with the remaining chives and the browned almonds. Serve at once.

CRUNCHY SESAME SQUID

SERVES 4

Squid is inexpensive and delicate in flavour. Most fishmongers sell the ready-cleaned white part or the ready-cut rings; if not they will happily remove the heads and innards, saving the tentacles for you if you wish.

FOOD VALUES	CARBOHYDRATE	FIBRE	FAT	KCALS/KJ
TOTAL	116.5G	5G	24G	864/3650
PER PORTION	29G	1G	6G	216/913

- 100 g/4 oz dry wholemeal breadcrumbs
- salt and freshly ground black pepper
- 2 tsp chopped fresh thyme or 1 tsp dried thyme
- 1 tbsp finely chopped parsley • grated rind of 1 lemon
- 2 tbsp sesame seeds (unroasted are best) • 50 g/2 oz plain flour
- 1 egg • 1 tbsp water
- 8–12 small to medium squid, cleaned and cut into rings (with or without tentacles, cut in pieces, as preferred) • lemon wedges to serve

1 Set the oven at 220°C, 425°F, gas 7.

2 Grease a baking tray. Mix the breadcrumbs, seasoning, thyme, parsley, lemon rind and sesame seeds on a large plate or shallow dish. Place the flour on a plate or in a dish.

3 Beat the egg with 1 tbsp water. Dip the squid rings one at a time in flour, then in egg and finally in the breadcrumb mixture.

Use a fork to shuffle each ring about in the crumb mixture so it is well coated, then place on the baking tray. If using the tentacles, coat them well too.

4 Bake the squid for about 15 minutes, until all the pieces are crisp and browned.

5 Serve at once, with lemon wedges for their juice.

COOK'S TIP
CLEANING SQUID

Hold the tentacles and head in one hand, then pull them away from the body sack, held firmly in the other hand. The innards will come away from the body with the tentacle part. Cut the tentacles off above the head if they are to be used. Discard the head and innards.

A long thin, transparent quill runs down inside the body – remove this if it has not come out. Rub off the mottled skin covering the body – this is fine and it comes away easily, sometimes taking off the small flaps with it. The flaps may be reserved once skinned or they may stay attached for slicing. Rinse the body and tentacles well inside and out, then dry them on absorbent kitchen paper. Slice the body into rings, usually about 1 cm/½ in wide. Cut the tentacles into two or three pieces.

OATY MACKEREL

SERVES **4**

A simple, delicious variation on traditional herrings in oatmeal.

FOOD VALUES	CARBOHYDRATE	FIBRE	FAT	KCALS/KJ
TOTAL	87G	8G	76G	1373/5742
PER PORTION	22G	2G	19G	343/1436

● *8 tbsp medium oatmeal* ● *salt and freshly ground black pepper*
● *4 small mackerel, gutted with heads off and boned* ● *a little lemon juice*

I Put the oatmeal on a plate and season it well. Hold one mackerel by its tail and sprinkle the flesh side with a little lemon juice. Press the fish on the oatmeal, flesh down and use a spoon to dust more oatmeal over the top of the fish. Press the oatmeal on well, then lay the mackerel on a grill rack. Repeat with the remaining mackerel.

2 Cook the mackerel under a moderately hot grill, allowing about 10 minutes on each side, until the oatmeal is browned and crisp and the fish is cooked through.

3 Serve piping hot, with thin bread and butter.

BAKED SPICY GOUJONS

SERVES **4**

A hint of curry-powder peps up otherwise plain goujons and baking rather than frying makes them more suitable for everyday eating. The coating procedure can be rather tedious, so it is worth coating a large batch when you have time, then open freezing them to pack for future use. Since the strips are thin they require only a few minutes extra cooking from frozen.

FOOD VALUES	CARBOHYDRATE	FIBRE	FAT	KCALS/KJ
TOTAL	59G	3G	24G	1179/5002
PER PORTION	15G	1G	6G	295/1251

• *4 large plaice or whiting fillets, skinned* • *50 g/2 oz plain flour*
• *salt and pepper* • *1 egg* • *1 tbsp water* • *75 g/3 oz fine dry breadcrumbs*
1½ tsp mild curry-powder • *lemon wedges to serve*

1 Set the oven at 220°C, 425°F, gas 7.

2 Grease a baking tray. Cut the fish fillets across into 1-cm/½-in wide strips, then dust them with the flour and plenty of seasoning.

3 Lightly beat the egg with 1 tbsp water in a shallow bowl. Mix the breadcrumbs with the curry-powder and a little seasoning – not too much – in a second shallow bowl.

4 Dip the fish strips in egg, then roll them in breadcrumbs and place them on the baking tray. Bake for 15 minutes, or until crisp and browned.

5 Serve at once, with lemon wedges for their juice. A light dip goes well with the goujons, or serve them with rice flavoured with a little lemon rind, a crisp salad and some natural yoghurt mixed with snipped chives.

COD AND COURGETTE GRATIN

SERVES **4**

You can substitute any white fish for the cod – try strips of whiting or plaice fillet, or chunks of haddock. Smoked fish – haddock, cod or coley fillet – are also particularly flavoursome.

FOOD VALUES	CARBOHYDRATE	FIBRE	FAT	KCALS/KJ
TOTAL	32G	7G	39G	1087/4562
PER PORTION	8G	2G	10G	272/1141

- 450 g/1 lb courgettes, trimmed and sliced
- 675 g/1½ lb cod fillet, skinned and cut in chunks
- 2 tbsp chopped parsley
- 2 tbsp chopped fresh tarragon or 1 tbsp dried tarragon
- 4 tbsp chopped chives or chopped spring onion
- salt and freshly ground black pepper ● 100 g/4 oz low-fat soft cheese
- 50 g/2 oz fresh wholemeal breadcrumbs
- 50 g/2 oz Cheddar cheese, grated

1 Set the oven at 180°C, 350°F, gas 4.

2 Arrange half the courgettes in the base of a shallow oven-proof dish – a gratin dish is ideal, a flan dish is too shallow and a casserole will do.

2 Make sure there are no bones in the fish, then place it on top of the courgettes. Sprinkle the parsley, tarragon and chives or spring onions over. Season well, then dot with the soft cheese. Top with the remaining courgettes.

3 Mix the breadcrumbs with the Cheddar cheese, then sprinkle the mixture over the courgettes. Bake for about one hour, until the topping is golden and the courgettes are just tender. Under the topping, the fish and lower layer of courgettes are baked in a herby, creamy sauce.

4 Serve at once, with baked or creamed potatoes, or a bowl of freshly cooked pasta.

FISH PARCEL

SERVES **4**

This recipe is derived from koulibiac – a classic pie of salmon and rice using a rich puff pastry crust. Filo pastry is thin, light and easy to use – it is not rich and fatty like other pastries but it is usually smothered with lots of melted butter before cooking. If you avoid brushing every pastry layer with fat when using filo it is ideal for frequent use in a balanced diet. Look out for it in the chiller cabinet or freezer in larger supermarkets. Small sheets measuring 18 x 35 cm/7 x 14 in are now common. The main type on sale until now was about 60 x 25 cm/24 x 10 in.

FOOD VALUES	CARBOHYDRATE	FIBRE	FAT	KCALS/KJ
TOTAL	113G	7G	65G	1586/6643
PER PORTION	28G	2G	16G	397/1661

- 50 g/2 oz long grain brown rice ● 1 small onion, finely chopped
- 200 ml/7 fl oz vegetable or fish stock
- salt and freshly ground black pepper ● 50 g/2 oz frozen peas
- 2 eggs, hard-boiled and chopped ● 4 large or 8 small sheets filo pastry
- 2–3 tbsp sunflower oil (or other light oil) ● 8 trout fillets

1 Place the rice, onion and stock in a small saucepan, adding a little salt if the stock is unseasoned. Bring to the boil, reduce the heat and cover the pan tightly. Cook very gently for 15 minutes, then add the peas to the pan but do not stir them in. Re-cover the pan and continue to cook for a further 15 minutes. Leave covered, off the heat, for 5 minutes.

2 Fork the rice and peas together, mix in the eggs and add a little pepper, then leave to cool slightly.

3 Set the oven at 200°C, 400°F, gas 6 and thoroughly grease a large baking tray.

4 Lay a double thickness of filo pastry on the tray, with the long side about 5 cm/2 in from the long edge of the baking tray and leaving the rest of the pastry overhanging the opposite edge of the tray. Brush the pastry on the middle of the tray with a little sunflower oil.

5 Lay the remaining filo in a double sheet overlapping the pastry already on the tray. The second layer of sheets should overhang the opposite side of the baking tray, making a four-layer thickness in the middle.

6 Lay four trout fillets on the middle of the pastry, then mound the rice mixture evenly over them. Top with the remaining trout fillets to cover the rice as evenly as possible. Brush the ends of the filo pastry with a little oil.

7 Fold one side of the pastry over to cover the filling. Brush the top of the pastry with a little oil, then fold the opposite side of pastry over the top to enclose the fish and rice completely in four thicknesses of pastry. Tuck the pastry edge under the parcel to make a neat edge. Make sure the pastry ends are well sealed by folding them over slightly.

8 Brush the parcel all over with a little oil, then bake for 30–40 minutes, or until the pastry is crisp and golden. Cut into thick slices to serve.

ACCOMPANIMENT IDEA – LIGHT TARTARE SAUCE

Mix 2 tbsp finely chopped parsley, 2 tbsp chopped gherkin, 1 tbsp chopped capers and 1 tbsp finely chopped onion with 4 tbsp mayonnaise. Stir in 250 ml/8 fl oz low-fat fromage frais and seasoning to taste.

This tartare-style sauce is far less rich and calorific than the traditional version made with all mayonnaise and it is delicious with the fish parcel.

MEAT AND POULTRY

Meat and poultry are among the main sources of protein in the average diet.

On a regular basis, avoid eating significant quantities of visible fat on meat. Chicken and turkey contain less fat than most meat, and farmed duck now has a lower fat content.

The sensible advice about eating meat and poultry is to balance it with alternate meals based on fish, beans, pulses and vegetables.

On a daily basis remember to use healthier cooking methods, such as grilling, stir-frying, braising or steaming, rather than frying and deep-frying; and serve high-fibre accompaniments – vegetables, salads, wholemeal rice or pasta – to complete the main course.

CRISP BAKED CHICKEN

SERVES **4**

Vary the herbs according to taste – thyme, parsley, marjoram, savory and rosemary are all suitable.

FOOD VALUES	CARBOHYDRATE	FIBRE	FAT	KCALS/KJ
TOTAL	34 G	5 G	29.5 G	877/3695
PER PORTION	9 G	1 G	7 G	219/924

- 4 chicken portions (quarters or breasts), skinned ● 1 tbsp oil
- 1 tbsp lemon juice ● 1 tbsp wholegrain mustard
- salt and freshly ground black pepper ● 1 tbsp dried sage
- 2 tbsp grated onion ● 75 g/3 oz fresh breadcrumbs

1 Set the oven at 190°C, 375°F, gas 5.

2 Place the chicken pieces in a greased ovenproof dish. Place the oil, lemon juice, mustard, plenty of seasoning, sage and onion in a screwtopped jar and shake well until everything is thoroughly combined.

3 Brush the chicken pieces generously with the mustard and onion mixture, ensuring that they are particularly well coated on top. Press the soft breadcrumbs on each chicken portion as it is brushed with the mixture to make a thick, even coating.

4 Bake the coated chicken for about 50–60 minutes, or until they are crisp and golden outside and thoroughly cooked through. Serve at once.

CHICKEN BIRIANI

SERVES 4

A biriani is a dish of rice cooked with other ingredients – it is most important that the chicken is cooked with the rice, not simply served on it, as this gives the dish its flavour. A sort of Indian risotto, I suppose!

FOOD VALUES	CARBOHYDRATE	FIBRE	FAT	KCALS/KJ
TOTAL	315G	9.5G	65G	2185/9204
PER PORTION	79G	2G	16G	546/2301

- 2 large onions, peeled • 2 garlic cloves, crushed
- 5-cm/2-in piece fresh root ginger, peeled • 2 tbsp garam masala
- 1 tsp turmeric • 4 tbsp natural yoghurt
- salt and freshly ground black pepper • 8 chicken thighs, skinned
- 3 tbsp oil • 2 bay leaves • 6 green cardamoms • 1 cinnamon stick
- 350 g/12 oz long-grain brown basmati rice (or ordinary brown rice if basmati is not available) • 900 ml/1½ pt water
- lemon wedges to serve • chopped fresh coriander to serve

1 Thinly slice 1 onion and set it aside. Cut the other onion into chunks, then purée it to a paste with the garlic, ginger, garam masala, turmeric and yoghurt. If you do not have a liquidizer or food processor, then grate the onion and ginger and mix with the other ingredients. Add plenty of seasoning, then spoon this mixture over the chicken thighs, spreading it evenly over them and turning them to coat all sides. Cover and chill for 1–24 hours, the longer the better.

2 Heat the oil in a large, heavy-based saucepan or flameproof casserole. Add the sliced onion, bay leaves and cardamoms, then cook, stirring often, until browned – about 20 minutes. Use a slotted spoon to remove half the onion from the pan and reserve it for garnish. Push the rest of the onion to one side.

3 Add the chicken portions, reserving the juices from marinating and brown them all over. Add the rice to the pan, sprinkling it down between the chicken. Tuck the cinnamon stick in between the chicken, then scrape all the marinating juices into the pan. Pour in 900 ml/1½ pt water. Bring to the boil, then reduce the heat and cover the pan tightly. Leave to cook gently for 30–35

minutes, until the rice has absorbed the water and the chicken is tender. The biriani should be moist.

4 Transfer the biriani to a serving dish, or serve it from the cooking pan, sprinkling the reserved onion over and adding some chopped fresh coriander, both for colour and its fresh flavour. Add lemon wedges for garnish – their juice should be squeezed over before the biriani is eaten.

COOK'S TIP

SPICY VARIATIONS

Use the basic spice purée for making a variety of Indian-style spiced chicken dishes. Here are a few ideas.

TANDOORI CHICKEN

Add the grated rind and juice of 1 lemon and ½ tsp chilli powder to the mixture. Marinate part-boned chicken breasts in the mixture for 24 hours. Bake at 220°C, 425°F, gas 7 for 40–50 minutes, until cooked through and well browned. Alternatively, grill slowly until evenly browned and cooked through.

CHICKEN TIKKA

Cut 4 boneless chicken breasts into large cubes. Marinate them in the spice mixture with 1 tbsp tomato purée stirred in, if liked. Thread the cubes on metal skewers and brush the marinade over them, then cook under a moderately hot grill until well browned and cooked through. These are also good cooked on a barbecue.

CHICKEN MASALA

Spread the paste mixture over chicken quarters and leave to marinate. Brown the chicken all over in a little oil, then add the marinade, bay, cinnamon and cardamoms as above. Pour in 100 ml/4 fl oz water and add seasoning, then bring to the boil. Reduce the heat, cover and cook gently for 45 minutes, turning the chicken once, until thoroughly cooked. Serve topped with toasted blanched almonds.

LAMB JARDINIÈRE

SERVES **4**

Noisettes of lamb are neat rounds of meat prepared by boning and rolling a rack of lamb, then tying it firmly at intervals so that the joint may be sliced between the string.

FOOD VALUES	CARBOHYDRATE	FIBRE	FAT	KCALS/KJ
TOTAL	103G	26G	45G	1207/5086
PER PORTION	26G	7G	11G	302/1272

- *8 noisettes of lamb or lamb cutlets*
- *salt and freshly ground black pepper*
- *1 tbsp chopped fresh rosemary or 2 tsp dried rosemary*
- *about 2 tbsp oil* • *2 leeks, sliced and washed*
- *225 g/8 oz baby carrots, scraped*
- *225 g/8 oz shelled broad beans or fresh peas* • *100 g/4 oz French beans*
- *450 ml/¾ pt lamb, vegetable or chicken stock*
- *2 tbsp plain flour* • *2 tbsp chopped fresh mint*

I Season the lamb well all over and sprinkle with the rosemary. Heat about 1 tbsp oil in a large flameproof casserole or heavy-based saucepan – you need just enough to thoroughly grease the base of the pan. Add the lamb and brown the pieces all over, then use a slotted spoon to remove them and set aside.

2 Add the leeks to the fat in the saucepan and cook, stirring, for 2 minutes before adding the remaining vegetables. Stir over medium heat for 2–3 minutes, then pour in the stock and heat until just boiling.

3 Replace the lamb on top of the vegetables and reduce the heat so that the liquid simmers gently. Cover the pan and cook for 10 minutes. Turn the lamb and cook for a further 10 minutes, until all the vegetables are tender but not too soft.

4 Use a slotted spoon to transfer the lamb and vegetables to a heated serving dish or plates. Beat the oil and flour together in a small basin. Whisking the simmering cooking liquid over medium heat, add the flour paste a little at a time. Whisk all the time to prevent lumps forming and the sauce should thicken as it boils. Boil for a minute or so, taste for seasoning, then pour the liquid over the meat and vegetables and serve at once, sprinkled with chopped mint.

PORK AND PINEAPPLE MEATBALLS

SERVES **4**

These unusual meatballs combine the ingredients used in sweet and sour pork, and the result is very tasty. We enjoyed the experience of eating the pineapple chunk encased in the meat mixture but the fruit can be chopped and mixed into the pork before shaping the meatballs.

FOOD VALUES	CARBOHYDRATE	FIBRE	FAT	KCALS/KJ
TOTAL	133G	10G	49G	1454/6127
PER PORTION	33G	2G	12G	364/1532

- 450 g/1 lb lean minced pork ● 6 spring onions, finely chopped
- 1 red or green pepper, seeded and finely chopped
- 50 g/2 oz fresh wholemeal breadcrumbs
- salt and freshly ground black pepper ● 2 eggs
- 227 g/8 oz can pineapple chunks in natural juice, drained
- 25 g/1 oz plain flour ● 1 tbsp water ● 75 g/3 oz dry breadcrumbs

1 Set the oven at 190°C, 375°F, gas 5. Grease a baking tray. Mix the pork, spring onions, pepper, breadcrumbs, seasoning and 1 egg. Pound the mixture well to combine all the ingredients evenly and bind them together.

2 Mop the pineapple chunks on a sheet of absorbent kitchen paper. Mark the meat mixture into four – each quarter should make three meatballs, making twelve in all.

3 Wash, then wet your hands. Take a portion of the meat mixture and flatten it into a patty on one hand. Place a pineapple chunk in the middle of the meat, then mould it around the fruit to enclose it completely in a smooth meatball. Shape the remaining mixture in the same way.

4 Place the flour on one plate and the breadcrumbs on a second plate. Beat the remaining egg with 1 tbsp water. Coat the meatballs in flour, then in the egg and lastly in the breadcrumbs. Place them on the baking tray as they are coated.

5 Bake the meatballs for 40 minutes, turning once, or until they are crisp and golden-brown outside and cooked through.

6 Serve at once, with Quick Tomato Sauce and rice, baked potatoes or pasta.

QUICK TOMATO SAUCE

Cook 1 finely chopped onion and a crushed garlic clove in 1 tbsp oil in a small saucepan, until soft but not browned. Stir in 2 tbsp tomato purée, 1 bay leaf, 1 thyme sprig, 2 x 400 g/14 oz cans chopped tomatoes and 100 ml/4 fl oz stock (chicken or vegetable). Bring to the boil, then reduce the heat and simmer the sauce, uncovered, for 15 minutes. Sieve or purée the sauce, or serve it chunky. Reheat the sauce if it is puréed.

STEAK AND VEGETABLE HOTPOT

SERVES **4**

This is a versatile, flavoursome stew: keep it very traditional by serving it with mashed, boiled or baked potatoes or use it as the base for a number of dishes.

FOOD VALUES	CARBOHYDRATE	FIBRE	FAT	KCALS/KJ
TOTAL	131G	34G	69G	1511/6336
PER PORTION	33G	8.5G	17G	378/1584

- *350 g/12 oz stewing or braising steak, diced ● 3 tbsp plain flour*
- *● salt and freshly ground black pepper ● 2 tbsp oil*
- *● 1 large leek, sliced and washed ● 1 large onion, chopped*
- *● 1 carrot, halved and sliced ● 1 bay leaf ● 2 parsley sprigs*
- *● 1 thyme sprig ● 600 ml/1 pt beef stock ● 2 parsnips, cut into chunks*
- *● ½ swede or celeriac, peeled and cut into chunks*
- *● 350 g/12 oz Brussels sprouts, halved unless very small*

1 The meat should be diced not cut in chunks. Toss it with the flour and plenty of seasoning. Heat the oil, then add the meat and cook it, stirring often, until sealed and lightly browned.

2 Add the leek, onion and carrot, then cook for 5 minutes, stirring. Tie the bay and herb sprigs into a bouquet garni and add it to the pan with the stock. Stir until the liquid is just simmering, then cover tightly and regulate the heat so that the stew simmers very gently. Boiling will toughen the meat. Cook for 2½ hours, stirring occasionally.

3 Add the parsnips and swede or celeriac to the stew, stir well and re-cover. Simmer for 15 minutes, add the sprouts and cook for a further 15 minutes, or until the parsnips and swede or celeriac are tender.

4 Taste and adjust the seasoning before serving piping hot.

VARIATIONS

WINTER PIE

The stew makes an excellent pie filling. Use wholemeal short crust pastry (see Peaches and Pears Pie, page 53), omitting the nuts, orange and sweetener and binding the dough with a little water) and cool the stew slightly before topping with pastry. Glaze with beaten egg or milk and bake at 200°C, 400°F, gas 6 for 30 minutes, until the pastry is cooked.

COBBLER

Use the stew to make a cobbler with the topping and cooking instructions for Pork and Cabbage Cobbler (page 37).

TACOS FILLER

Serve the stew in tacos shells and top with some grated cheese.

SAUCED LIVER STIR-FRY

SERVES **4**

Take advantage of good quality frozen vegetables or fresh produce in season to transform traditional liver and bacon into a thoroughly modern dish. Serve this in a ring of mashed potatoes or on a bed of cooked rice.

FOOD VALUES	CARBOHYDRATE	FIBRE	FAT	KCALS/KJ
TOTAL	132G	11.5G	63G	1455/6102
PER PORTION	33G	3G	16G	364/1526

- 350 g/12 oz lamb's liver ● 4 tbsp plain flour
- salt and freshly ground black pepper
- 2 tsp chopped fresh sage or 1 tsp dried sage ● 1 tbsp oil
- 100 g/4 oz rindless smoked bacon, roughly chopped
- 1 large onion, halved and thinly sliced
- 2 celery sticks, cut into short thin strips
- 225 g/8 oz carrots, cut into short thin strips
- 225 g/8 oz fine French beans, halved
- 250 ml/8 fl oz chicken or vegetable stock ● dash of Worcestershire sauce

1 Trim the liver of any sinews and membrane, then rinse and dry it on absorbent kitchen paper. Cut it horizontally into thin slices, then across into fine strips. Place the strips in a basin and sprinkle the flour, salt, pepper and sage over. Mix well to coat all the liver in flour and seasonings.

2 Heat the oil in a large frying-pan or wok. Add the bacon and cook, stirring, until it is lightly browned. Add the liver, shaking off any excess flour (but reserve it for later) and stir-fry until lightly browned and just cooked. Use a slotted spoon to remove the liver from the pan.

3 Add the onion, celery and carrots to the pan and stir-fry over medium heat until the onion is thoroughly softened – about 20 minutes. Add the beans and cook for 3 minutes, then stir in any leftover flour from the liver and pour in the stock. Bring to the boil, stirring all the time.

4 Reduce the heat and replace the liver. Mix in the Worcestershire sauce and taste for seasoning, then simmer gently for 5 minutes, until the liver is hot and the vegetables are cooked but not soft. Serve at once.

WHEATEN MINCE WITH APPLE

SERVES **4**

Not only is this a good way of making mince go a little further, it also gives the mixture a delicious nutty flavour and satisying texture; what's more it increases the fibre value of the dish.

FOOD VALUES	CARBOHYDRATE	FIBRE	FAT	KCALS/KJ
TOTAL	183G	28G	49G	1622/6830
PER PORTION	46G	7G	12G	406/1708

- 1 tbsp oil ● 450 g/1 lb lean minced pork ● 1 large onion, chopped
- 2 celery sticks, chopped ● 1 carrot, diced ● 1 bay leaf
- 2 tsp chopped fresh sage or 1 tsp dried sage
- 2 dessert apples (225 g/8 oz), peeled, cored and diced
- 225 g/8 oz cracked wheat ● 450 ml/3/4 pt water
- salt and freshly ground black pepper ● a little grated nutmeg
- plenty of chopped parsley

1 Heat the oil in a flameproof casserole or heavy-based saucepan. Add the pork and cook it over medium heat, stirring often, until it is well browned. Drain off any excess fat from the meat.

2 Add the onion, celery and carrot. Cook, stirring occasionally, for about 15 minutes or until the vegetables are lightly cooked. Add the bay, sage, apple, wheat, plenty of seasoning and a little nutmeg, then mix well before stirring in the water.

3 Bring just to the boil, reduce the heat and cover the pan. Leave to simmer for 20 minutes, or until most of the liquid has been absorbed, leaving the meat tender, the wheat plump and the mixture juicy.

4 Stir in chopped parsley and taste for seasoning before serving.

5 A crisp salad or lightly cooked vegetables are sufficient accompaniments for a light meal: add some cooked rice, a baked potato or crusty bread for a more substantial main course.

BRAISED KIDNEYS WITH CRUNCHY BACON

SERVES **4**

FOOD VALUES	CARBOHYDRATE	FIBRE	FAT	KCALS/KJ
TOTAL	78G	7G	53G	1302/5475
PER PORTION	19.5G	2G	13G	326/1369

- 450 g/1 lb lambs' kidneys ● 3 tbsp plain flour
- salt and freshly ground black pepper ● 2 tbsp oil
- 1 onion, halved and thinly sliced ● 225 g/8 oz mushrooms, sliced
- 1 tbsp wholegrain mustard (or other mild made mustard)
- ½ tsp dried thyme ● 450 ml/¾ pt chicken stock
- 225 g/8 oz lean rindless bacon ● 2 tbsp chopped parsley

1 Rinse the kidneys and mop them on absorbent kitchen paper. Remove the membrane that covers them, if necessary, then cut them in half and use kitchen scissors to snip out the white core. Toss the prepared kidneys in the flour with plenty of seasoning.

2 Heat the oil in a flameproof casserole or heavy saucepan. Add the kidneys and lightly brown them all over, then stir in the onion and cook gently for 10 minutes, until slightly softened.

3 Stir in the mushrooms, mustard and thyme, with any leftover flour from coating the kidneys. Cook for a minute, stirring to combine the ingredients, then pour in the stock. Heat, stirring, until the liquid just boils, reduce the heat and simmer gently, uncovered, for 20 minutes.

4 Meanwhile, grill the bacon under a moderately hot grill until it is crisp and golden. Transfer to absorbent kitchen paper to drain and cool slightly. Crumble the bacon into small pieces and mix it with the parsley.

5 Taste the kidneys for seasoning, then transfer them to a warm serving dish or plates and sprinkle with the bacon mixture. Serve straight away.

LAMB AND POTATO CURRY

SERVES **4**

Potatoes are delicious spiced – they absorb and counteract the flavours of spices perfectly. In this dish they extend the comparatively small meat content.

FOOD VALUES	CARBOHYDRATE	FIBRE	FAT	KCALS/KJ
TOTAL	241G	20G	56G	1787/7542
PER PORTION	60G	5G	14G	447/1886

- *2 onions, chopped • 5-cm/2-in piece fresh root ginger, peeled*
- *2 garlic cloves • 2 tbsp lemon juice • 2 tbsp ground coriander*
- *1 tbsp ground cumin • 1 tsp ground fenugreek • 1 tsp turmeric*
- *½ tsp chilli powder • ½ tsp salt*
- *350 g/12 oz lean boneless lamb, diced • 2 tbsp oil • 1 bay leaf*
- *1 cinnamon stick • 4 green cardamoms • 2 tbsp tomato purée*
- *600 ml/1 pt water • 1.25 kg/2½ lb potatoes, cubed*
- *2 tbsp chopped mint or fresh coriander*

1 Purée 1 onion, the ginger, garlic, lemon juice, coriander, cumin, fenugreek, turmeric, chilli and salt to a paste in a liquidizer or food processor. Alternatively, grate the onion and ginger, crush the garlic and combine these with the remaining ingredients.

2 Place the lamb in a large basin and pour the paste over, then mix well to coat all the meat in paste. Cover and leave to marinate for at least 2 hours, or up to 24 hours in the refrigerator.

3 Heat the oil in a large flameproof casserole or heavy-based saucepan. Add the remaining onion, bay leaf, cinnamon stick and cardamoms, then cook gently, stirring often, for 15 minutes. Stir in the tomato purée and pour in the water. Add the lamb and all its marinade. Stir well and heat until just simmering. Cover and cook gently for 1½ hours, until the lamb is tender.

4 Taste the cooking liquid for seasoning before adding the potatoes and stir in extra salt if necessary. Add the potatoes, mix well, cover and continue to simmer gently for a further 30 minutes. Stir occasionally to prevent the potatoes sticking. At the end of the cooking time the potatoes should be very tender but not mushy.

5 Serve the curry sprinkled with fresh mint and coriander, with rice and a Cucumber Raita.

CUCUMBER RAITA

Peel and dice ½ cucumber (about 225 g/8 oz). Place it in a colander and sprinkle with salt, then leave to stand over a bowl for 20 minutes. Mop the cucumber on absorbent kitchen paper before mixing it with 250 ml/8 fl oz natural yoghurt. Sprinkle with a little chopped fresh mint and a light dusting of chilli powder or garam masala, if liked. Serve freshly prepared.

HOME-MADE BURGERS

MAKES **8**

FOOD VALUES	CARBOHYDRATE	FIBRE	FAT	KCALS/KJ
TOTAL	49G	8G	48G	932/3854
PER BURGER	6G	1G	6G	117/482

- *450 g/1 lb lean minced beef • 1 onion, grated*
- *1 tsp dried mixed herbs, marjoram or sage • 2 tbsp chopped parsley*
- *1 egg • salt and freshly ground black pepper*
- *dash of Worcestershire sauce • 100 g/4 oz fresh wholemeal breadcrumbs*
- *a little oil*

1 Place the meat in a bowl. Add the onion, herbs, egg, seasoning and Worcestershire sauce, then mix well until all the ingredients are thoroughly combined. Add the breadcrumbs and pound the mixture well to combine them evenly with the seasoned meat.

2 Wash your hands, then wet them and shape the mixture into eight burgers, each measuring about 7.5–10 cm/3–4 in across.

Brush the burgers with a little oil and grill them for about 5 minutes on each side, regulating the heat so they cook through without overbrowning. Serve at once.

VARIATIONS
LAMB BURGERS

Use minced lamb, flavoured with marjoram, rosemary or mint.

PORK BURGERS

Use lean minced pork. Add a grated eating apple if you like.

SERVING SUGGESTIONS

- Serve the burgers in toasted buns with salad and gherkins.
- Stir-fry a mixture of vegetables – celery, carrots, onions and cabbage – and top them with the burgers.

ONE-POT MEALS

I have to admit that one-pot meals are my favourites for everyday and to share with friends, so I hope you will agree that these dishes are easy to serve and satisfying – ideal for all the family and equally delicious for informal entertaining.

They range from old-fashioned dinners to international specialities. Offer wholemeal or crusty bread to mop up the juices and make a crisp side salad if you like to add a fresh, light aspect to the meal. Some of the dishes are ideal for cooking ahead – the Lentil Layer or Cottage Surprise both spring to mind. If you do cook ahead, always cool the food as quickly as possible, then cover it and keep it chilled until it comes to be reheated. Make sure it is thoroughly heated before serving and never reheat food more than once.

BOILED BACON WITH MINTY CABBAGE

SERVES **4**

One of my mother's specialities, this is a delicious, traditional way of cooking a joint of bacon and vegetables. The result is flavoursome, full of food value and light because there is no rich sauce. Leftover cold cooked bacon is perfect for salads, sandwiches or as a topping for baked potatoes. Save the stock for making soup – a pot full of mixed vegetables with pearl barley or pasta makes another satisfying meal.

FOOD VALUES	CARBOHYDRATE	FIBRE	FAT	KCALS/KJ
TOTAL	214G	25G	31G	1637/6907
PER PORTION	53.5G	6G	8G	409/1727

(allowing 100 g/4 oz lean cooked meat)

- *boned and rolled bacon joint for boiling (about 1.2 kg/2½ lb in weight)*
- *1 large onion* ● *225 g/8 oz carrots, cut in chunks* ● *1 bay leaf*
- *a few parsley sprigs* ● *2 cloves* ● *1 blade of mace*
- *1 kg/2¼ lb potatoes, peeled and halved if large*
- *1 small green cabbage, trimmed and separated into leaves*

MINT SAUCE

- *4 tbsp chopped fresh mint* ● *4 tbsp boiling water*
- *4 tbsp cider vinegar* ● *sweetener to taste*

1 Weigh the joint. Calculate the cooking time at 30 minutes per 450 g/1 lb plus an extra 30 minutes. With modern curing methods joints do not usually have to be soaked before cooking as they are less salty; however, it is as well to check with the butcher.

2 Place the joint in a large saucepan with the onion, carrots, bay leaf, parsley, cloves and mace. Add cold water to cover the joint and bring to the boil over medium heat. As the water begins to simmer, and during the first few minutes of boiling, scum will rise to the surface: use a slotted spoon or larger metal spoon to skim this off. Regulate the heat so that the water simmers and cover the pan. Cook for all but the final 20 minutes.

3 For the mint sauce, stir the mint and boiling water together in a small dish or basin. Add the cider vinegar and stir in sweetener to taste. Cover and set aside.

4 Add the potatoes to the joint 20 minutes before the end of cooking and continue to simmer. Transfer the meat from the pan to a large heated serving dish, with the potatoes and carrots. If any of the potatoes are not quite tender, leave them in the pan while cooking the cabbage. Cover the meat and keep hot.

5 Bring the cooking stock to the boil, then add the cabbage and boil for 3–5 minutes, until cooked to taste.

6 Meanwhile, slice the required amount of meat, discarding the rind and excess fat.

7 Drain the cabbage in a colander over a large bowl to catch the stock or use a slotted spoon to transfer the cabbage into a colander over a bowl. Roughly chop the cabbage and arrange on the dish with the potatoes and sliced meat.

8 Spoon a little mint sauce over the meat and vegetables and serve at once. Offer the remaining mint sauce separately.

BACON HOTPOT WITH
DELICIOUS DUMPLINGS

SERVES **4**

Whether you loved or loathed them, forget about suet dumplings; what we have here are light, low-fat dumplings with a worthy fibre content. I'm an unapologetic dumpling fan, so I was delighted with the results.

FOOD VALUES	CARBOHYDRATE	FIBRE	FAT	KCALS/KJ
TOTAL	328G	55G	134G	2955/12527
PER PORTION	82G	14G	33G	739/3132

- 1 tbsp oil ● 450 g/1 lb boneless gammon or bacon, cubed, or bacon offcuts
- 1 large onion, chopped ● 2 tbsp plain flour
- 600 ml/1 pt stock (bacon, vegetable or chicken)
- 250 ml/8 fl oz unsweetened apple juice ● 225 g/8 oz carrots, sliced
- 225 g/8 oz parsnips, cubed ● 450 g/1 lb swede or celeriac, cubed
- salt and freshly ground black pepper
- 450 g/1 lb Brussels sprouts, halved if large

DUMPLINGS

- 100 g/4 oz self-raising flour ● 1 tsp baking-powder
- 100 g/4 oz fresh wholemeal breadcrumbs ● 50 g/2 oz rolled oats
- 2 tbsp chopped parsley ● 2 tsp chopped fresh sage or 1 tsp dried sage
- 4 spring onions, chopped ● ½ tsp salt
- 100 g/4 oz low-fat soft cheese (Light Philadelphia or Shape)
- 100 ml/4 fl oz skimmed milk

1 Heat the oil, add the bacon and brown the pieces lightly, then add the onion and continue cooking for about 10 minutes, or until the onion is softened. Stir in the flour and pour in the stock. Bring to the boil stirring, then pour in the apple juice.

2 Add the carrots, parsnips and swede or celeriac with seasoning – do not add too much salt at this stage. Reduce the heat so that the liquid is just simmering, cover and continue to cook gently for 30 minutes.

3 For the dumplings, mix the flour, baking-powder, breadcrumbs, oats and parsley with the sage and spring onions. Stir in ½ tsp salt and make a well in the middle of the mixture. Beat the cheese with the milk, then add it to the dry ingredients and mix together thoroughly.

4 Divide the mixture in half, then shape each half into four round dumplings. Add the sprouts to the hotpot and stir, then place the dumplings on top and cover tightly. If the dumplings are too high for the lid, tent foil over the top of the pan, tucking it around the rim to keep in the steam.

5 Simmer for 20 minutes, until the dumplings are risen and cooked through. Use a slotted spoon to transfer the dumplings to serving plates, then ladle the bacon and vegetable mixture beside them. Serve at once.

COOK'S TIP
THE STOCK ALTERNATIVE

If your casserole is too full to accommodate the dumplings, add them to a pan of just simmering stock and cook gently for 20 minutes. Do not boil the stock since the dumplings will tend to disintegrate – keep the liquid just about simmering.

Use a slotted spoon to remove the dumplings from the pan and save the stock for making soup.

TURKEY AND LEEK OATY

SERVES **4**

Boneless chicken breast may be substituted for the turkey, if preferred; however, this is a good way of using frozen diced turkey meat. Leftovers from a roast bird may be used: dice the meat and add it to the sauce instead of frying it at the beginning of cooking. The savoury crumble topping may also be used on a variety of bases, including fish and meat. The oats are a valuable source of fibre as well as adding a delicious texture and flavour to this dish.

FOOD VALUES	CARBOHYDRATE	FIBRE	FAT	KCALS/KJ
TOTAL	283G	31G	58G	2180/9212
PER PORTION	71G	8G	14G	545/2303

- 1 tbsp oil ● 450 g/1 lb uncooked boneless, skinned turkey, diced
- 450 g/1 lb potatoes, diced ● 450 g/1 lb leeks, sliced and washed
- 1 bay leaf ● 3 tbsp plain flour ● 450 ml/¾ pt turkey or chicken stock
- 100 g/4 oz mushrooms, sliced (optional)
- 225 g/8 oz frozen mixed vegetables
- salt and freshly ground black pepper ● 50 g/2 oz plain flour
- 25 g/1 oz butter or margarine ● 100 g/4 oz rolled oats
2 tsp chopped fresh sage or 1 tsp dried sage ● 4 spring onions, chopped
- grated rind of 1 lemon

1 Heat the oil in a flameproof casserole or heavy-based saucepan. Add the turkey and cook over medium to high heat, stirring all the time, until the pieces are lightly browned. Add the potatoes and cook for 2 minutes, stirring all the time.

2 Stir in the leeks and bay leaf, then cook, stirring, for 5 minutes, until they are softened. Stir in the flour and gradually pour in the stock. Bring to the boil, stirring, then add the mushrooms (if used), frozen mixed vegetables and seasoning. Remove the pan from the heat.

3 Set the oven at 180°C, 350°F, gas 4.

4 If necessary, transfer the turkey mixture to an ovenproof dish.

5 Place the flour in a bowl and rub in the butter. Stir in the oats, sage, spring onions and lemon rind with a little seasoning. Sprinkle the oat mixture over the turkey and bake for 40–45 minutes, until the topping is golden and cooked through. Serve piping hot.

SINGLE PORTION SUGGESTION

Brown a boneless chicken breast all over in the oil, over medium heat, then dice it – don't worry if it is not completely cooked at this stage. Place the chicken in an ovenproof dish and pour in a small can of cream of chicken soup. Add some frozen mixed vegetables and sliced mushrooms. Instead of the above topping, cut a thick slice of bread into small dice and mix it with 25 g/1 oz oats, 1 chopped spring onion and a good pinch of sage. Sprinkle over the chicken mixture, then dot with a little butter, margarine or trickle 1 tsp oil over. Bake as above, until golden and cooked.

LENTIL LAYER

SERVES **4**

Turn this into a tempting, well-balanced, meatless dish by replacing the ham with 2 x 400 g/14 oz cans chick-peas, drained.

FOOD VALUES	CARBOHYDRATE	FIBRE	FAT	KCALS/KJ
TOTAL	251G	28G	49G	2070/8726
PER PORTION	63G	7G	12G	518/2182

- 2 onions, chopped • 350 g/12 oz red lentils
- 900 ml/1½ pt vegetable stock • knob of butter or margarine
- salt and freshly ground black pepper • 1 tbsp oil
- 6 celery sticks, chopped
- 225 g/8 oz cut French beans, frozen or blanched fresh (lightly cooked runner-beans may be used instead) • 225 g/8 oz cooked ham, diced
- 40 g/1½ oz dry white breadcrumbs • 2 tbsp Parmesan cheese

1 Place 1 onion in a saucepan with the lentils. Add the stock and bring to the boil. Reduce the heat, cover the pan tightly and cook gently for 25 minutes, until all the stock has been absorbed and the lentils are tender. Beat well until the lentils are smooth apart from the onion, adding the butter or margarine and seasoning to taste.

2 Set the oven at 190°C, 375°F, gas 5.

3 Grease an ovenproof dish and spread half the lentil mixture in it. Heat the oil in a heavy-based saucepan. Add the remaining onion and the celery, cover and cook over medium heat, stirring occasionally, for about 20 minutes, or until the onion is softened.

4 Stir the beans and ham into the celery mixture, with a little seasoning, then re-cover and cook for 5 minutes. Spread this mixture over the lentil base, patting it down evenly with the back of a spoon. Top with the remaining lentils, which should be spread out in an even layer.

5 Mix the breadcrumbs and Parmesan. Sprinkle the mixture over the top of the lentils and bake for 20 minutes, or until golden brown, crisp and hot through.

6 Serve at once: the celery should still have a bit of bite to contrast with the soft lentils and ham.

COTTAGE SURPRISE

SERVES **4–6**

FOOD VALUES	CARBOHYDRATE	FIBRE	FAT	KCALS/KJ
TOTAL	246G	33G	115G	2421/10151
PER PORTION (4)	61.5G	8G	29G	605/2538
PER PORTION (6)	41G	5.5G	19G	404/1692

- 1 cauliflower, broken into florets • 450 g/1 lb leeks, sliced
- 50 g/2 oz butter or margarine • 40 g/1½ oz plain flour
- 300 ml/½ pt milk • salt and freshly ground black pepper
- 4 eggs, hard-boiled and roughly chopped
- 100 g/4 oz Cheddar cheese, grated
- 1 kg/2¼ lb potatoes, boiled and mashed

1 Set the oven at 180°C, 350°F, gas 4.

2 Place about 5 cm/2 in water in a large saucepan and bring it to the boil. Add the cauliflower and leeks and bring back to the boil. Boil rapidly for 3–5 minutes, until the cauliflower is just tender. Drain well in a colander over a bowl and save 300 ml/ ½ pt of the cooking water.

3 Melt half the butter or margarine in a saucepan. Stir in the flour, then cook for a minute before stirring in the reserved cooking liquid. Gradually pour in the milk and bring to the boil, stirring all the time. Add seasoning to taste and three-quarters of the cheese.

4 Place the cauliflower and leeks in an ovenproof dish. Stir the eggs into the sauce, then pour it over the cauliflower mixture. Beat the reserved butter into the mashed potatoes, with pepper to taste. Spread the potatoes over the vegetables and mark the top with a fork. Sprinkle with the remaining grated cheese.

5 Bake for about 40 minutes, until the topping is golden and crisp. Serve freshly baked.

PORK AND CABBAGE
COBBLER

SERVES **4**

A cobbler has a scone topping. Here the mixture of pork, red cabbage and apple is turned into a hearty meal by adding a crown of savoury scones.

FOOD VALUES	CARBOHYDRATE	FIBRE	FAT	KCALS/KJ
TOTAL	245G	42G	127G	2765/11590
PER PORTION	61G	11G	32G	691/2898

- 1 tbsp oil ● 450 g/1 lb lean minced pork ● 1 large onion, chopped
- 1 garlic clove, crushed (optional) ● 1 tbsp fennel seeds (optional)
- 2 tbsp plain flour ● 2 dessert apples, peeled, cored and chopped
- 350 ml/12 fl oz chicken or vegetable stock
- 675 g/1½ lb red cabbage, shredded
- salt and freshly ground black pepper

TOPPING

- 225 g/8 oz plain wholemeal flour ● 3 tsp baking-powder
- 50 g/2 oz margarine ● 3 tbsp grated Parmesan cheese
- 50 g/2 oz Cheddar cheese, grated ● 2 tbsp chopped parsley
- 150 ml/¼ pt milk plus extra for glazing

1 Heat the oil, add the pork and stir over medium heat until lightly browned. If the meat yields a lot of fat, pour some off at this stage, then add the onion, garlic and fennel (if used). Cook, stirring, for 10 minutes to soften the onion slightly before stirring in the flour, apples and stock.

2 Bring to the boil, stir in the cabbage and salt and pepper, then simmer for 10 minutes. Transfer the mixture to an oven-proof dish.

3 Set the oven at 220°C, 425°F, gas 7.

4 For the topping, mix the flour and baking-powder in a bowl, then rub in the margarine. Add some seasoning, then stir in the Parmesan, Cheddar and parsley. Mix in enough milk to bind the ingredients in a soft dough. Turn the dough out on a lightly floured surface, and roll it out to about 2.5 cm/1 in thick. Cut out 12 small round scones, re-rolling the trimmings as necessary.

5 Overlap the scones on top of the pork mixture, then brush them with a little milk. Bake for 20–25 minutes, until the scone topping is well risen and golden brown. Serve freshly baked.

SMOKED HADDOCK HOTCHPOTCH

SERVES **4**

This is the perfect winter's meal for anyone who enjoys fish – serve it simple, with lots of warmed crusty bread to mop up juices left on the plate!

FOOD VALUES	CARBOHYDRATE	FIBRE	FAT	KCALS/KJ
TOTAL	234G	21G	46G	2072/8755
PER PORTION	59G	5G	12G	518/2189

- 2 tbsp oil ● 1 onion, chopped ● 225 g/8 oz carrots, diced
- 4 celery sticks, halved lengthways and sliced
- 1 kg/2¼ lb potatoes, cut in chunks
- salt and freshly ground white or black pepper ● 1 bay leaf
- 600 ml/1 pt fish stock ● 225 g/8 oz frozen peas ● 600 ml/1 pt milk
- 675 g/1½ lb smoked haddock fillet, skinned and cut in chunks
- 3 tbsp chopped parsley

1 Heat the oil in a large, heavy-based saucepan. Add the onion, carrots and celery, then cook, stirring, for 15 minutes, until the onion is softened slightly. Stir in the potatoes with a little seasoning and the bay leaf. Pour in the stock and bring to the boil. Reduce the heat, cover the pan and simmer for 15 minutes.

2 Add the frozen peas to the mixture and cook for a further 10 minutes. Stir in the milk and bring back to simmering point. Reduce the heat and add the fish with the parsley, then simmer very gently for 10 minutes or until the fish is just cooked. Taste for seasoning and serve piping hot.

SINGLE PORTION SUGGESTION

Use 1 small onion, 1 carrot and 1 medium potato. If you do not want to make fish stock, use half a stock cube or use all skimmed milk instead of half stock and half milk. Buy a small, thick portion of smoked haddock fillet rather than a tail end. Instead of the frozen peas, you may like to sprinkle a roughly chopped hard-boiled egg over the soup before serving.

VEGETABLES AND SIDE-DISHES

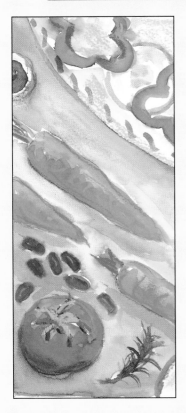

Include plenty of fresh or frozen vegetables in your daily diet, cooking them lightly (boiling, steaming or stir-frying) or serving them raw. Try grated carrots with unsweetened orange juice and a little olive oil, shredded cabbage mixed with grated apple and a few walnuts, or diced tomatoes with spring onions and lightly cooked French beans.

Home-made salad dressings are tasty and more versatile than bought types. Use a light salad oil or olive oil, cider vinegar for a less harsh result or Balsamic vinegar for a rich, dark dressing. Orange, grapefruit or lemon juice is excellent in place of vinegar. Add mustard, herbs, garlic, onion, sesame seeds or peanut butter for flavour; use a sweetener in place of sugar. Fromage frais or yoghurt make good creamy dressings.

When it comes to making sauces on a regular basis use semi-skimmed milk if you want to keep the fat level low. In addition, it is worth noting that children under the age of five years should not have their fat intake restricted.

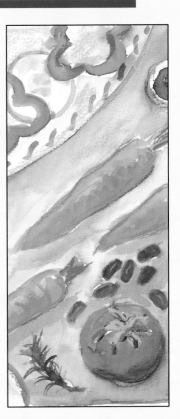

LEEK AND PARSNIP ROLL

SERVES **4**

This is delicious, economical and smart enough to serve for a dinner party. Serve it with Quick Tomato Sauce (see page 28), minted new potatoes and French beans or a salad for a light main course; or serve it alone with a delicate salad garnish for a tasty first course.

FOOD VALUES	CARBOHYDRATE	FIBRE	FAT	KCALS/KJ
TOTAL	108G	26G	70G	1272/5325
PER PORTION	27G	6G	17G	318/1331

- 350 g/12 oz parsnips, cubed ● 1 tbsp oil ● 350 g/12 oz leeks, chopped
  ● 2 tbsp plain flour ● 3 eggs, separated
- salt and freshly ground black pepper ● 225 g/8 oz low-fat soft cheese
  ● 2 tbsp chopped parsley ● 1 tbsp chopped fresh tarragon or mint

1 Line and grease a 23 x 33 cm/9 x 13 in Swiss-roll tin.

2 Set the oven at 190°C, 375°F, gas 5.

3 Place the parsnips in a saucepan and pour in water to cover. Bring to the boil, then reduce the heat slightly, cover and cook for about 15 minutes, until the parsnips are tender. Drain and mash well.

4 Heat the oil, add the leeks and cook, stirring, for about 20 minutes, or until softened.

5 Add half the leeks to the parsnips. Stir them in well, then sift the flour over and beat it in followed by the egg yolks. Whisk the whites until stiff, then use a metal spoon to fold them into the parsnip mixture.

6 Spread the mixture in the prepared tin and bake for about 25 minutes, until firm and golden brown.

7 Meanwhile, lay out a clean tea-towel covered with a piece of grease-proof paper.

8 Place the remaining leeks over very gentle heat to keep them hot. A couple of minutes before the roll is ready, stir the soft cheese into the leeks in the pan, remove from the heat and add the herbs with seasoning to taste.

9 Turn the roll out on to the prepared paper and tea-towel. Remove the lining paper from the cooked roll and spread the cheese mixture over the top. Using the paper and tea-towel as a guide, roll up the baked mixture to enclose the filling in the same way as a Swiss roll.

10 Slice and serve at once.

MARROW RAGOUT

SERVES 4

This is a good way of turning marrow into a delicious supper dish or vegetarian meal. Making your own bouquet garni is important – it is better to change the herbs according to availability than to compromise with a mixture of dried herbs. You can, of course, substitute courgettes for the marrow.

FOOD VALUES	CARBOHYDRATE	FIBRE	FAT	KCALS/KJ
TOTAL	89G	19G	63G	1058/4473
PER PORTION	22G	5G	16G	265/1118

- 3 tbsp olive oil ● 2 onions, chopped ● 4 celery sticks, chopped
- 2 carrots, diced ● 2 garlic cloves, crushed ● 1 bouquet garni
- 4 tbsp tomato purée ● 400 g/14 oz can chopped tomatoes
- salt and freshly ground black pepper
- 675 g/1½ lb marrow, peeled, seeded and cubed
- 75 g/3 oz fresh wholemeal breadcrumbs ● 2 tbsp chopped parsley
- 75 g/3 oz cheese, grated

1 Heat the oil in a flameproof casserole. Add the onions, celery, carrots, garlic and bouquet garni. Stir well until sizzling, then cover and cook over medium heat for 20 minutes, stirring once.

2 Stir in the tomato purée and canned tomatoes with plenty of seasoning. Bring to the boil. Add the marrow cubes and mix well. Reduce the heat so that the mixture barely simmers, cover and cook very gently for 1 hour, stirring occasionally. The marrow cubes should be tender but not mushy.

3 Set the oven at 200°C, 400°F, gas 6.

4 Mix the breadcrumbs, cheese and parsley, then sprinkle the mixture over the marrow. Bake for 20–30 minutes, until crisp and golden on top, then serve at once. If preferred, the topping may be cooked under a grill heated to a medium setting, until crisp and golden-brown.

SPICY TWO PEAS

SERVES **4**

With apologies for the title but recommendations to try this one if you like spicy food. Serve this spicy mixture of green peas and chick-peas as an accompaniment for an Indian-style main course or as a nutritious vegetarian main dish.

FOOD VALUES	CARBOHYDRATE	FIBRE	FAT	KCALS/KJ
TOTAL	97G	28G	37G	877/3670
PER PORTION	24G	7G	9G	219/918

- 2 tbsp oil ● 1 garlic clove, crushed ● 1 onion, chopped
- 1 tbsp cumin seeds ● 2 tbsp crushed coriander seeds ● 1 tbsp poppy seeds
- 1 tbsp mustard seeds ● salt and freshly ground black pepper
- 400 g/14 oz can chick-peas, drained ● 225 g/8 oz frozen peas
- 100 ml/4 fl oz water ● 2 tbsp chopped fresh mint or coriander
- natural yoghurt to serve (optional)

1 Heat the oil, then add the garlic, onion, cumin, coriander, poppy and mustard seeds. Sprinkle with salt and pepper to taste. Cook, stirring, over a medium heat for about 15 minutes, until the onion is softened.

2 Stir in the frozen peas and add the water. Bring to the boil, then simmer quite fast, uncovered, for 5 minutes. Stir in the chick-peas and continue to cook until the liquid has evaporated, leaving the peas cooked and the mixture hot.

3 Sprinkle the mint or coriander over and serve at once, with a little yoghurt swirled in if liked.

MARROW AND SWEETCORN CRUNCH

SERVES **4**

Another marrow recipe, because if you have a large marrow you are likely to get at least two very different meals from it – without having to resort to stuffed marrow. Semolina and cheese topping adds a pleasing crunch to this dish.

FOOD VALUES	CARBOHYDRATE	FIBRE	FAT	KCALS/KJ
TOTAL	217G	16G	118G	2145/8972
PER PORTION	54G	4G	30G	536/2243

- 675 g/1½ lb marrow, peeled, seeded and cubed
- 1 small onion, finely chopped ● 1 tsp ground mace
- salt and freshly ground black pepper
- 1 bouquet garni ● 2 tsp olive oil
- 340 g/12 oz can sweetcorn, drained ● 100 g/4 oz walnuts, chopped
- 2 tbsp semolina ● 4 tbsp grated Parmesan cheese
- 4 tbsp dry white breadcrumbs

1 Place the marrow, onion, mace and seasoning in a large flameproof casserole and mix well. Add the bouquet garni and the oil and mix again to coat the vegetables. Heat until the mixture begins to sizzle, then put a tight-fitting lid on the pan and cook gently for 25 minutes. Regulate the heat so that the mixture just murmurs in the pan.

2 Add the sweetcorn, mix well and cook for a further 5 minutes, with the lid on the pan. The marrow should be tender but firm.

3 Mix the nuts, semolina and Parmesan, then sprinkle the mixture over the vegetables and put under a moderately hot grill until evenly browned. If the mixture is browned too quickly it will become dark or burn, a lower heat is more successful. Serve straight away.

BEETROOT AND CHEESE PATTIES

MAKES **8**

I love fresh beetroot and I think these are scrumptious – if you like beetroot as a vegetable I am sure you will agree. If fresh cooked beetroot is not available, buy the vacuum-packed long-life type which does not have vinegar added. Make a large batch, if you like, and freeze them for future use.

FOOD VALUES	CARBOHYDRATE	FIBRE	FAT	KCALS/KJ
TOTAL	162G	22G	63G	1428/5998
PER PATTY	20G	3G	8G	179/750

- 25 g/1 oz butter or margarine • 1 small onion, finely chopped
- 25 g/1 oz plain flour • 150 ml/¼ pt milk
- salt and freshly ground black pepper • 100 g/4 oz Cheddar cheese, grated
- 200 g/7 oz fresh breadcrumbs
- 450 g/1 lb cooked beetroot, peeled and grated

1 Melt the butter or margarine in a saucepan. Add the onion and cook, stirring, for 10 minutes. Stir in the flour, then gradually pour in the milk and bring to the boil, stirring all the time, to make a very thick sauce.

2 Off the heat, add seasoning and the cheese to the sauce. Stir in 50 g/2 oz of the breadcrumbs and the beetroot. Mix well to ensure all the ingredients are thoroughly combined.

3 Set the oven at 220°C, 425°F, gas 7 and grease a baking tray.

4 Place the remaining breadcrumbs on a large plate or sheet of foil. Pat the beetroot mixture into a neat shape, mark into quarters, then cut it into eight equal portions.

5 Use a spoon to scoop out one portion of the mixture (the quantity does not have to be exact) and drop it neatly on the breadcrumbs. Use a damp palette knife to flatten the mixture slightly, then sprinkle breadcrumbs all over the top and use your hands to press the mixture into a neat round cake, about 2.5 cm/1 in thick and 6 cm/2½ in in diameter. Press plenty of breadcrumbs on the mixture to coat the outside of the patty thickly and to prevent it sticking to your hands. Place on the baking tray. Repeat with the remaining portions of mixture.

6 Bake the patties for 10–15 minutes, until crisp and well browned outside. Serve at once.

COOK'S TIP
GRILLING PATTIES

If you want to avoid heating the oven, place the tray of patties well away from the heat source under a moderately hot grill and cook slowly until thoroughly crisp and browned. Use a palette knife or slice to turn the patties and grill the second side.

ONION AND
CHESTNUT GRATIN

SERVES **4**

This is an unusual accompaniment for roasts, such as pork, beef or lamb, and ideal for adding a new dimension to the Christmas turkey. On a more day-to-day basis, serve it with grilled bacon, gammon or sausages.

FOOD VALUES	CARBOHYDRATE	FIBRE	FAT	KCALS/KJ
TOTAL	370G	40G	86G	2443/10267
PER PORTION	92G	10G	22G	611/2567

- *675 g/1½ lb chestnuts ● 675 g/1½ lb pickling onions, peeled*
- *1 bay leaf ● 600 ml/1 pt milk ● 25 g/1 oz butter or margarine*
- *25 g/1 oz plain flour ● salt and freshly ground black pepper*
- *a little grated nutmeg ● 2 tbsp chopped parsley*
- *40 g/1½ oz fresh breadcrumbs*
- *100 g/4 oz Stilton cheese, finely crumbled*

1 Wash the chestnuts, then slit their shells with the point of a knife. Place them in a saucepan and cover with water. Bring to the boil, reduce the heat and cover the pan. Simmer for 10 minutes, then drain and peel the chestnuts.

2 Place the onions, chestnuts, bay leaf and milk in a saucepan. Bring to the boil over medium heat, taking care not to allow the milk to boil over. Reduce the heat just as the milk is boiling and stir the vegetables, then three-quarters cover the pan and leave to simmer very gently for 40 minutes, or until the onions are tender. Stir often to prevent the mixture burning.

3 Drain the vegetables, reserving the milk, and place them in a dish to go under the grill. Melt the butter or margarine, stir in the flour, then slowly add the milk, stirring, and bring to the boil. Cook, stirring, for 3 minutes. Add plenty of seasoning, a little nutmeg and the chopped parsley, then pour the sauce over the onions and chestnuts.

4 Mix the breadcrumbs and Stilton, then sprinkle the mixture evenly over the vegetables. Grill until bubbling hot and golden brown, then serve at once.

MUSHROOM AND TOMATO SAUCE

SERVES 4

Ladle this quick and easy sauce over piping hot pasta and offer freshly grated Parmesan cheese to sprinkle on top.

FOOD VALUES	CARBOHYDRATE	FIBRE	FAT	KCALS/KJ
TOTAL	36G	14G	48G	647/2728
PER PORTION	9G	4G	12G	162/682

- 4 tbsp olive oil ● 2 garlic cloves, crushed
- 450 g/1 lb mushrooms, sliced ● 1 bunch spring onions, chopped
- salt and freshly ground black pepper ● 1 bay leaf
- 2 x 400 g/14 oz cans chopped tomatoes ● 2 tbsp tomato purée
- handful of fresh basil sprigs, stalks discarded and leaves shredded

1 Heat the oil in a large frying-pan or heavy-based saucepan. Add the garlic, mushrooms, spring onions, seasoning and bay leaf. Cook, stirring often, over medium heat for about 20 minutes, or until the mushrooms are well cooked and much of the liquor they yield has evaporated.

2 Add the canned tomatoes and stir in the purée, then bring to the boil and reduce the heat. Simmer for 3 minutes, then taste for seasoning. Stir in the basil and serve the sauce.

CREAMED BEANS AND HAM

SERVES **4**

Cooking broad beans with savory, and serving them with cream and ham is a classic method. Here is an adaptation using low-fat soft cheese. The beans make a splendid supper dish on their own, with some wholemeal bread and butter or chunks of crusty French bread; or they may be ladled over pasta or into split baked potatoes. Alternatively, offer them as a first course or as a side-dish for plain grilled poultry or meat.

FOOD VALUES	CARBOHYDRATE	FIBRE	FAT	KCALS/KI
TOTAL	62G	31G	50G	1135/4766
PER PORTION	16G	8G	13G	284/1192

- *450 g/1 lb shelled broad beans* • *2 savory or thyme sprigs*
- *25 g/1 oz butter or margarine, or 2 tbsp olive oil* • *1 onion, chopped*
- *225 g/8 oz lean cooked ham, diced*
- *salt and freshly ground black pepper*
- *100 g/4 oz low-fat soft cheese (such as Light Philadelphia or Shape)*
- *2 tbsp chopped parsley or 1 tbsp chopped fresh tarragon*

1 Cook the beans with the savory or thyme in boiling water to cover for 10–15 minutes, until tender and cooked to taste. Melt the butter or margarine, or heat the oil, and add the onion. Cook, stirring often, for about 15 minutes, or until the onion is very tender, keeping the heat moderate to low to avoid browning the onion.

2 Add the ham, drained beans and seasoning to the onion. Stir over medium heat for 2 minutes, then stir in the low-fat cheese and cook over low heat for a minute until the cheese has melted. Sprinkle with parsley or tarragon and serve at once.

CREAMED CELERY SAUCE

SERVES 4

A creamy, low-fat sauce for serving with pasta, either as a topping for spaghetti or tagliatelle, or to layer with lasagne.

FOOD VALUES	CARBOHYDRATE	FIBRE	FAT	KCALS/KJ
TOTAL	90G	10G	39G	930/3901
PER PORTION	22G	3G	10G	233/975

- 1 head celery ● 2 tbsp olive oil ● 1 onion, chopped
- 1 garlic clove, crushed (optional) ● 1 carrot, diced ● 1 bay leaf
- 3 tbsp plain flour ● 250 ml/8 fl oz dry white wine
- 250 ml/8 fl oz vegetable stock ● salt and freshly ground black pepper
- 100 g/4 oz low-fat soft cheese (Light Philadelphia or Shape type)
- 1–2 tbsp chopped fresh tarragon or a handful of basil sprigs, trimmed and shredded (optional)

1 Trim the celery, discarding the root end and tips of the stalks. Reserve the leafy part and chop it finely as it can be added to the sauce. Separate the stalks, scrub them, then dice each one. This is not difficult – cut them lengthways into three or four strips, then across into dice.

2 Heat the oil in a large, heavy-based saucepan. Add the onion, garlic (if used), carrot, bay leaf and celery. Stir well over medium heat for 5 minutes, then cover the pan and cook gently for 15 minutes to soften the vegetables.

3 Stir in the flour, then gradually pour in the wine and stock. Bring to the boil, reduce the heat and simmer gently, uncovered, for 20 minutes, stirring occasionally. Add seasoning to taste and stir in the low-fat cheese. Do not boil. Remove from the heat and add the tarragon or basil, then serve at once.

SAVOURY SPROUTS
WITH AVOCADOS

SERVES **4**

Brussels sprouts have a very frumpy image, mainly from their association with soggy overcooked vegetables served as part of poorly cooked, so-called celebration, dinners that run up to Christmas. Lightly boiled or steamed, so that they still have a bit of crunch, sprouts are good with traditional meals and they are also versatile ingredients for the more adventurous cook. Serve this tempting mixture as a side-dish for grilled poultry or meat, or use it to top freshly cooked pasta, rice or other grains, such as buckwheat or couscous.

FOOD VALUES	CARBOHYDRATE	FIBRE	FAT	KCALS/KJ
TOTAL	64G	41G	129G	1564/6488
PER PORTION	16G	10G	32G	391/1622

- 675 g/1¹/₂ lb Brussels sprouts ● 1 tbsp oil ● 1 onion, chopped
- 1 garlic clove, crushed (optional)
- 3 tbsp pine kernels or split blanched almonds ● 1 tsp dried oregano
- 3 tbsp raisins ● salt and freshly ground black pepper
- 2 ripe avocados ● juice of ¹/₂ lemon ● 2 tbsp chopped mint or parsley

1 Halve the sprouts unless they are very small. Add them to a small amount of boiling water, bring back to the boil and cook for 2–3 minutes, then drain and set aside.

2 Heat the oil. Add the onion, garlic, if used, pine kernels, oregano and raisins with a good dash of seasoning. Cook over moderate heat, stirring often, for about 15 minutes, or until the onion is softened.

3 Meanwhile, halve the avocados and remove their stones, then quarter the flesh and remove the peel. Cut the flesh into chunks and toss them in the lemon juice.

4 Add the sprouts to the onion mixture and cook, stirring, for about 2 minutes, until they are really hot. Stir in the avocados and parsley or mint, then cook, stirring, for about 3 minutes, or until the avocado is hot and slightly creamy. Serve at once.

PUDDINGS AND DESSERTS

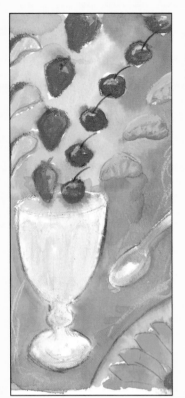

I tend to think of desserts as special because we do not eat "pudding" every day. Fresh fruit, a fruit salad or low-fat yoghurt are the best options.

I have found that making delicious desserts to suit my mother's diabetic diet and please everyone else around the table is not difficult with a little fore-thought. Fruit pies, flans and crumbles using whole-meal flour and a sweetener are all good candidates. Cooked dessert apples have an excellent flavour, but they do take longer to become tender, so precook them before using them in a pie.

Try mixing sharp fruits, for example rhubarb or gooseberries, with mellow ingredients like banana or strawberries.

The range of sweeteners available means that you can create a wide variety of puddings without using sugar at all.

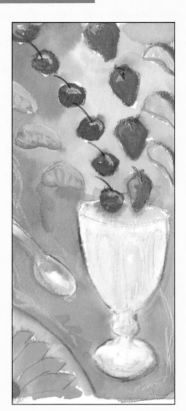

PINEAPPLE SOUFFLÉ

SERVES **6**

FOOD VALUES	CARBOHYDRATE	FIBRE	FAT	KCALS/KJ
TOTAL	97 G	4 G	87 G	1413/5907
PER PORTION	16 G	1 G	14.5 G	236/985

(Above values do not include cream for decoration)

- *1 quantity Confectioner's Custard (see Apple and Orange Trifle, page 50), without orange rind* ● *4 tsp gelatine* ● *4 tbsp water*
- *432 g/15 oz can crushed pineapple in natural juice* ● *2 egg whites*
- *100 g/4 oz walnuts, chopped*

1 Prepare a soufflé dish: tape a thick band of doubled grease-proof paper around the side of a 900 ml/1½ pt soufflé dish. The paper should stand above the rim of the dish by 5 cm/2 in. Secure it at the top, bottom and middle with sticky tape.

2 Make up the Confectioner's Custard and leave it to cool at room temperature but do not chill.

3 Sprinkle the gelatine over 4 tbsp cold water in a basin and leave for 15 minutes until sponged, or swollen and spongy in appearance. Stand the basin over hot water and stir until the gelatine has dissolved completely.

4 Stir the gelatine into the pineapple and leave until just begin-ning to thicken, then stir it into the custard. Whisk the egg whites until they stand in stiff peaks but they should not be "dry". Fold the whites into the mixture, then turn it into the prepared dish. Chill until set.

5 Untape the paper and slide the blade of a knife between the paper and the soufflé as you roll the band of paper away. Press the nuts on the side of the soufflé.

FRANGIPANE FRUIT TART

SERVES **8**

This is a real treat – in summer top it with fresh strawberries, raspberries or apricots; later in the year use quartered plums or sliced exotic fruit (kiwi or star fruit, mangoes), or unsweetened canned fruit in natural juice.

FOOD VALUES	CARBOHYDRATE	FIBRE	FAT	KCALS/KJ
TOTAL	183G	33G	178.5G	2625/10946
PER PORTION	23G	8G	22G	328/1368

- 100 g/4 oz wholemeal flour • 50 g/2 oz plain flour
- 75 g/3 oz butter or margarine • 75 g/3 oz almonds, chopped
- 4 tbsp water • grated rind of 1 orange

FRANGIPANE FILLING

- 25 g/1 oz plain flour • 2 egg yolks • 1/2 tsp natural vanilla essence
- 1/2 tsp oil of bitter almonds • 300 ml/1/2 pt milk
- 100 g/4 oz ground almonds • sweetener to taste
- 100 ml/4 fl oz fromage frais

TOPPING

- 450 g/1 lb strawberries, hulled and halved if large

1 Mix the wholemeal and white flours in a bowl. Rub in the butter or margarine, then stir in the chopped almonds and just enough water to bind the ingredients – about 4 tbsp. Gather the dough together and roll it out large enough to line a 23 cm/9 in loose-bottomed flan tin. Chill for at least 30 minutes if possible.

2 Set the oven at 200°C, 400°F, gas 6.

3 Prick the pastry base all over with a fork, then line it with grease-proof paper and baking beans. Bake for 20 minutes, then remove the paper and ceramic baking beans or dried peas. Cook for a further 5–10 minutes, until the pastry is cooked through. Remove from the oven and allow to cool.

4 For the filling, place the flour in a basin. Add the egg yolks, vanilla essence and almond oil. Stir in a little of the milk to combine the ingredients in a smooth paste. Heat the remaining milk until hot but not quite boiling, then pour it into the paste, stirring all the time.

5 Pour the milk mixture back into the pan and cook over low to moderate heat, stirring all the time. At first the mixture will begin to seem very lumpy – don't be alarmed, this is all part of the fun of making pastry cream or Confectioner's Custard, simply carry on stirring vigorously as though your life depends on it (the success of your custard certainly does). By the time the mixture boils it will be very thick; reduce the heat to very low so that it barely simmers and beat it well so that it becomes smooth. Cook for 3 minutes – this is important to overcome the gluey flavour of raw flour.

6 Remove the pan from the heat and cover the surface of the mixture with wetted grease-proof paper, then leave it to cool. When cold, beat the mixture really well – using an electric beater if possible – until smooth. Beat in the almonds and sweetener to taste. Do not add too much sweetener – remember that the mixture should be slightly sweet and creamy. Then fold in the fromage frais. Chill well.

7 Spread the frangipane in the pastry case and arrange the strawberries on top. Serve the flan within an hour of filling.

COOK'S TIP
FLAVOUR NATURALLY

The quality of the flavouring is all important to the success of this flan. Synthetic vanilla and almond flavourings will make it taste very nasty; instead look for natural vanilla and almond flavourings or oil of bitter almonds. Most large supermarkets offer them, otherwise try wholefood shops, delicatessens or herbalists.

GREEN FRUIT IN STRAWBERRY SAUCE

SERVES **6**

This is a refreshingly tangy – keep it that way by adding only the minimum of sweetener to the sauce. Use ripe dessert gooseberries instead of the very bitter cooking gooseberries.

FOOD VALUES	CARBOHYDRATE	FIBRE	FAT	KCALS/KJ
TOTAL	149G	27G	3G	622/2633
PER PORTION	25G	4.5G	0.5G	104/439

- 675 g/1½ lb dessert gooseberries, topped and tailed
- 450 g/1 lb strawberries, hulled • 225 g/8 oz seedless green grapes

1 Place the gooseberries and half the strawberries in a saucepan. Cover and cook gently for 15–20 minutes, or until the gooseberries are tender and the strawberries make a flavoursome sauce. Crush the strawberries with a spoon, then transfer to a serving dish.

2 Purée the remaining strawberries in a food processor, blender or by pressing them through a sieve, then stir them into the gooseberry mixture. Add the grapes and serve or leave until completely cold before serving.

3 Fromage frais or plain yoghurt goes well with the fruit.

APPLE AND ORANGE TRIFLE

SERVES **6**

FOOD VALUES	CARBOHYDRATE	FIBRE	FAT	KCALS/KJ
TOTAL	250G	16G	233G	2040/8622
PER PORTION	42G	3G	39G	340/1437

- 675 g/1½ lb dessert apples (Cox's Orange Pippin or a full-flavoured type), peeled, cored and cut in chunks • 2 tbsp water
- 1 layer Sandwich Cake (page 57) • grated rind and juice of 1 orange
- 3 tbsp dry sherry

CONFECTIONER'S CUSTARD

- 25 g/1 oz plain flour • 2 egg yolks • 1 tsp natural vanilla essence
- 300 ml/½ pt milk • sweetener to taste
- 250 ml/8 fl oz fromage frais, yoghurt or half-fat whipping cream
- toasted flaked almonds to decorate

1 Place the apples in a saucepan and add 2 tbsp water. Heat gently, covered, for about 15 minutes, stirring occasionally. As the apples soften, the heat may be increased, continue cooking until the apples are reduced to a purée – this takes 30–40 minutes for eating-apples, with frequent stirring. It yields a delicious purée which does not require added sugar.

2 Break the cake into pieces and place them in a trifle bowl – the cake may be used from frozen. Mix the orange juice and sherry, then sprinkle it over the cake. Top with the apple purée.

3 For the custard, place the flour in a basin. Add the egg yolks and vanilla essence. Stir in a little of the milk to combine the ingredients in a smooth paste. Heat up the remainder of the milk until hot but not quite boiling, then pour it into the paste, stirring all the time.

4 Pour the milk mixture back into the pan and cook over a low to moderate heat, stirring all the time, as for Frangipane Fruit Tart (see page 44). By the time the mixture boils it will be very thick. Reduce the heat to very low so that it barely simmers and beat it well so that it becomes smooth. Cook for 3 minutes – this is important to overcome the flavour of raw flour.

5 Stir in the orange rind. Remove the pan from the heat and cover the surface of the mixture with wetted grease-proof paper, then leave it to cool. When cold, beat the mixture really well – using an electric beater if possible – until smooth. Beat in the sweetener to taste. Do not add too much sweetener – remember

that the mixture should be slightly sweet and creamy. Then fold in the fromage frais, yoghurt or cream and spread the custard over the apples. Chill well. Top with toasted flaked almonds before serving.

COOK'S TIP
TRIFLE IDEAS

Use this as a basis for making different trifles, substituting fresh raspberries, strawberries or other fruit for the apples. If you do want to sweeten the fruit, add sweetener to the orange-and-sherry mixture, then spoon that over once the fruit has been arranged on top of the cake. For a jellied trifle, make up a fruit-juice jelly (see previous recipe) and pour that over both fruit and sponge-cake. Allow to set before adding the custard topping.

PEAR AND LEMON CHEESECAKE

SERVES **8**

I have used biscuits from the following chapter as a base for the cheesecake; however you may substitute unsweetened breakfast cereal, such as bran flakes or muesli (the latter makes a very good base, in fact). If you own a freezer, try to get into the swing of batch-baking your own biscuits and cakes for it is significantly more economical, superior to buying sugar-free commercial products and always handy for making quick puddings.

FOOD VALUES	CARBOHYDRATE	FIBRE	FAT	KCALS/KJ
TOTAL	165G	7G	97G	1752/7268
PER PORTION	21G	1G	12G	219/909

- 1 batch baked Simple Biscuits (page 64), or 100 g/4 oz savoury wholemeal crackers with bran (see Cook's Tip below)
- 50 g/2 oz butter or margarine, melted ● 1 tbsp cocoa powder
- 2 tbsp sweetener

TOPPING

- 450 g/1 lb curd cheese or quark ● grated rind and juice of 1 lemon
- 450 g/1 lb firm pears ● about 4 tbsp sweetener
- 3 tsp powdered gelatine ● 4 tbsp water
- 300 ml/½ pt double cream substitute (Elmlea), fromage frais or Greek-style yoghurt ● small bunches of black and green grapes for decoration

1 Place the biscuits or crackers in a polythene bag and use a rolling-pin to crush them – or do this in a food processor. Melt the butter in a medium to large saucepan and add the cocoa powder. Cook, stirring, for a minute, then add the biscuit crumbs and remove from the heat. Mix thoroughly to coat all the biscuits in butter and cocoa.

2 Press the biscuit mixture into the base of a 23 cm/9 in loose-bottomed deep flan tin or cake tin. Chill.

3 Beat the curd cheese or quark with the lemon rind.

4 Place the lemon juice in a saucepan. Peel, core and dice the pears, then add them to the lemon juice and mix well. Cook the pears gently, stirring often, for about 10 minutes, or until they are very tender but not squashy. The very light cooking brings out their flavour. Cool slightly, then stir the pears and juice into the cheese mixture with sweetener to taste.

5 Sprinkle the gelatine over 4 tbsp water in a small basin. Set aside for 15 minutes, or until it is sponged, that is swollen to appear like a sponge. Place the basin in a saucepan of hot water and stir until the gelatine has dissolved completely.

6 Cool the gelatine, stirring, for 2–3 minutes, then stir it into the pear mixture. If using Elmlea, whip it until it stands in soft peaks. Fold the Elmlea, fromage frais or yoghurt into the pear mixture and pour it over the biscuit base. Smooth the top and chill the cheesecake for several hours, until set.

7 Slide a knife around the inside of the tin and stand the loose bottom on a storage jar. Carefully lower the side of the tin, then transfer the cheesecake to a serving platter. Arrange the grapes in small bunches around the edge, alternating black and green.

COOK'S TIP
THE CRACKER BASE

The savoury crackers make a delicious base for the cheesecake – combined with the cocoa and sweetener they have an excellent, slightly sweetened flavour. Avoid any highly salted or flavoured crackers and buy the plainest type available. The wholemeal/bran content is important for the flavour. This crumb mixture may also be used for pressing into a flan tin for making a flan case to fill with fruit.

PLUM RING

SERVES **8**

FOOD VALUES	CARBOHYDRATE	FIBRE	FAT	KCALS/KJ
TOTAL	118G	11G	70G	1280/5366
PER PORTION	15G	1G	9G	160/671

CHOUX PASTE

- *150 ml/¼ pt water* ● *50 g/2 oz butter or margarine*
- *75 g/3 oz plain flour* ● *2 eggs* ● *25 g/1 oz flaked almonds for topping*

FILLING

- *450 g/1 lb plums, halved and stoned* ● *grated rind and juice of 1 orange*
- *300 ml/½ pt fromage frais* ● *2 tbsp sweetener*

1 Set the oven at 220°C, 425°F, gas 7.

2 Grease a baking tray. Pour the water into a medium-sized saucepan. Add the butter or margarine, then place the saucepan over low heat until the fat has melted completely. Turn the heat right up to maximum and bring the mixture to the boil as quickly as possible.

3 Immediately the liquid boils, tip in all the flour, stir well and turn off the heat or remove the pan from the hob. Stir the flour mixture until it forms a smooth ball of paste. Do not beat it and stop mixing as soon as it forms a paste, then put on one side to cool for 5 minutes.

4 Lightly beat the eggs, then gradually beat them into the paste. Beat well after every addition and continue beating when all the egg is incorporated to make the paste smooth and glossy.

5 Spoon or pipe the paste into a ring on the baking tray – it should measure 18 cm/7 in across (see Cook's Tip).

6 Sprinkle the almonds over the top and bake for 15 minutes, then reduce the oven temperature to 180°C, 350°F, gas 4 and cook for a further 15–20 minutes, until well puffed, golden and firm to the touch.

7 Slice the choux ring in half horizontally and cool it on a wire rack as soon as it is cooked, or it will quickly lose its crisp texture.

8 Place the plums, orange rind and juice in a saucepan. Cook gently for 5–10 minutes, depending on the ripeness of the fruit, to slightly soften the plums. Cool.

9 Place the bottom of the choux ring on a serving platter. Stir the fromage frais with sweetener to taste, then spread it over the ring. Top with the plums – they will not all fit on, so save the remainder to serve with individual portions – then place the top of the choux ring in place. Serve within an hour of filling, adding any extra plums to plates when the ring is cut in portions.

COOK'S TIP
JUDGING THE RING

It is fairly easy to judge the size and shape of rings when you follow this sort of recipe often; however, for best results, cut a sheet of non-stick cooking parchment and draw a circle of the required size on it. Use a heavy black pencil or pen. Put the paper, pen-side down on the tray and you will be able to see the mark of the ring to use as a guide for spooning or piping the choux paste.

CHOUX PASTE SUGGESTIONS

ORANGE ÉCLAIRS

Pipe 12 éclairs using a 1.5 cm/¾ in nozzle and bake at 220°C, 425°F, gas 7 for 15 minutes, then at 180°C, 350°F, gas 4 for about 25 minutes. Split and cool on a wire rack. Stir 4 tbsp Orange Freezer Marmalade (page 70) into 300 ml/½ pt fromage frais and add sweetener to taste. Use the orange mixture to fill the buns.

CHOCOLATE ÉCLAIRS

Make as above. Fill with fromage frais, whipped Elmlea or whipped cream. Spread the top of each eclair generously with Chocolate Spread (page 69) and dust with a little extra cocoa powder if liked. Serve soon after filling and topping – not quite traditional but delicious!

ICE-CREAM

SERVES **8**

FOOD VALUES	CARBOHYDRATE	FIBRE	FAT	KCALS/KJ
TOTAL	60G	1G	74G	1051/4383
PER PORTION	7.5G	TRACE	9G	131/548

- *1 quantity Confectioner's Custard (see Apple and Orange Trifle, page 47, made without orange rind)*
- *300 ml/½ pt half-fat double cream or double non-dairy cream*
- *1 tsp natural vanilla flavouring* ● *4 tbsp powdered sweetener*

1 Make the Confectioner's Custard following the recipe instructions. The custard should be sweeter than when used for trifle as it will seem less so when frozen. Whip the cream with the vanilla until it stands in soft peaks. Stir in the sweetener, then fold the cream into the custard and immediately turn the mixture into a freezer container.

2 Freeze until half-frozen, then beat the mixture well or whizz it in a food processor to remove all the ice crystals. Freeze overnight.

3 Soften the ice-cream in the refrigerator for around 15 minutes before serving.

FLAVOURING ICE-CREAM

CHOCOLATE

Add 2 tbsp cocoa powder to the flour when making the custard.

COFFEE

Dissolve 1 tbsp instant coffee in 2 tbsp boiling water and add to the custard before checking for sweetness.

BANANA

Add 4 mashed bananas, mixed with 1 tbsp lemon juice, to the custard before folding in the cream – this is delicious.

PEACHES AND PEARS PIE

SERVES **6**

FOOD VALUES	CARBOHYDRATE	FIBRE	FAT	KCALS/KJ
TOTAL	216G	38G	112.5G	1961/8183
PER PORTION	36G	6G	19G	327/1364

- 425 g/15 oz can peach slices in natural juice
- 4 ripe pears, peeled, cored and sliced ● grated rind of 1 orange

PASTRY

- 100 g/4 oz wholemeal flour ● 50 g/2 oz margarine
- 100 g/4 oz walnuts, chopped ● grated rind and juice of 1 orange
- 4 tbsp sweetener

1 Set the oven at 200°C, 400°F, gas 6.

2 Mix the peaches and their juice with the pears in a pie dish or ovenproof dish.

3 Place the flour in a bowl, then rub in the margarine. Stir in the walnuts, orange rind and sweetener with enough orange juice to bind the mixture.

4 Roll out the nut pastry slightly larger than the top of the pie dish. Cut a strip and dampen the edge of the dish, then press the strip on the rim of the dish. Dampen the pastry rim and lift the rest of the pastry over. Seal the edges and use any trimmings to decorate the pie – cut out shapes or leaves and dampen them to keep them in place.

5 Brush with a little milk and bake for about 30 minutes, or until the pastry is cooked and browned. Serve piping hot.

LAST-MINUTE CHRISTMAS PUDDING

SERVES **6–8**

Omitting the sugar from Christmas pudding does not lessen its eating quality – of course it is less rich, but many people prefer it this way. However, since the sugar acts as a preservative, this "sugar-free" pudding is not intended for long storage except by freezing. It may be made up to 2 weeks ahead and stored in the refrigerator or up to 6 months in advance and frozen. Remember that the high proportions of dried fruit mean that this pudding does have a high fruit-sugar content.

FOOD VALUES	CARBOHYDRATE	FIBRE	FAT	KCALS/KJ
TOTAL	413G	35G	68G	2450/10348
PER PORTION (6)	69G	6G	11G	408/1725
PER PORTION (8)	52G	4G	8.5G	306/1294

- 225 g/8 oz raisins • 175 g/6 oz currants
- 50 g/2 oz ready-to-eat prunes, chopped
- 100 g/4 oz ready-to-eat dried apricots, chopped • 1 carrot, grated
- 2 dessert apples, peeled, cored and grated • 100 g/4 oz ground almonds
- 25 g/1 oz wholemeal flour • 100 g/4 oz fresh wholemeal breadcrumbs
- 1 tsp ground cinnamon • 1 tsp ground mixed spice
- 1/2 tsp grated nutmeg • grated rind and juice of 1 orange
- grated rind of 1 lemon • 1 egg • 2 tbsp brandy

1 Mix all the ingredients together in the order listed, stirring well to ensure that they are thoroughly combined.

2 Grease a 1.1 L/2 pt pudding basin and spoon the mixture into it, pressing down well with the back of a spoon. Cut a large piece of doubled grease-proof paper and grease one side, then use this to cover the basin, with the greased side facing down. Cover with foil and tie in place.

3 Steam the pudding over boiling water for 5 hours, adding fresh boiling water from the kettle to the saucepan regularly to prevent it boiling dry. Uncover the pudding and allow to cool. Then either cover with fresh grease-proof, pack in a polythene bag and place towards the bottom of the refrigerator for up to 2 weeks. Or, to freeze, turn out the cool pudding and pack it in a polythene bag. Label and freeze. Thaw overnight or for several hours in a cool room, then replace in a greased basin for reheating.

4 To serve the pudding, cover as before and steam for 2 hours. Serve with custard flavoured with brandy or brandy sauce. Frangipane cream (see Frangipane Fruit Tart, page 49) is also delicious with the pudding.

ACCOMPANIMENTS FOR CHRISTMAS PUDDING

BRANDY SAUCE

Blend 40 g/1½ oz cornflour to a paste with a little milk taken from 600 ml/1 pt. Heat the remaining milk, then pour it on the cornflour mixture, stirring. Pour the mixture back into the milk and bring to the boil, stirring all the time. Simmer for 3 minutes, stirring. Remove from the heat and add sweetener to taste with a knob of butter and 4 tbsp brandy. Stir well, then serve at once.

BRANDY-FLAVOURED CUSTARD

Make the Confectioner's Custard as for the Apple and Orange Trifle, omitting the orange rind. Do not allow the custard to cool before stirring in the fromage frais with 2–3 tbsp brandy.

ST CLEMENT'S CREAMY JELLY

SERVES **4**

It is important to leave the jelly until it is just beginning to set before folding in the fromage frais or yoghurt, otherwise it will separate out.

FOOD VALUES	CARBOHYDRATE	FIBRE	FAT	KCALS/KJ
TOTAL	54G	3G	1G	366/1589
PER PORTION	13.5G	1G	0.5G	92/397

- grated rind and juice of 4 oranges • grated rind and juice of 2 lemons
- 6 tbsp sweetener • 3 tsp gelatine • 4 tbsp water
- 300 ml/½ pt fromage frais or natural yoghurt
- segments from 1 orange to decorate (optional)

1 Heat the orange and lemon rind and juice together in a small saucepan until boiling, then remove from the heat and cool slightly before stirring in the sweetener. Set aside to cool.

2 Sprinkle the gelatine over 4 tbsp water in a small basin. Set aside for 15 minutes until sponged, or swollen and spongy in appearance, then set the basin over hot water and stir until the gelatine has dissolved completely.

3 Stir the gelatine mixture into the fruit juices. When cold place in the refrigerator to chill. When the mixture is just beginning to set, so that it is syrupy in texture, fold in the fromage frais or yoghurt. Divide the mixture between four glass dishes and chill until set. Decorate with orange segments, if liked, before serving.

> **COOK'S TIP**
>
> #### JELLY IDEAS
>
> Unsweetened fruit juices make terrific jellies – try any of the mixtures sold in cartons to create a wide variety of colourful desserts. Most juice from cartons is quite sweet enough and there should be no need to add sweetener. Add fresh fruit to the jelly or make layers of different jellies for a colourful effect.

SAVARIN

SERVES **8**

Traditional savarin is soaked in rum syrup but this recipe uses a sweetener substitute which works very well. Fill the middle with the customary fruit salad or vary the dessert by serving it with hot poached fruit as suggested below. The baked, unsoaked savarin freezes well.

FOOD VALUES	CARBOHYDRATE	FIBRE	FAT	KCALS/KJ
TOTAL	262G	22G	116G	2450/10276
PER PORTION	33G	2.8G	14.5G	306/1285

- *225 g/8 oz strong white flour* ● *½ tsp salt* ● *1 sachet easy-blend yeast*
- *250 ml/8 fl oz milk* ● *4 eggs* ● *100 g/4 oz butter, melted*
- *4 tbsp white rum* ● *2 tbsp water* ● *3 tbsp sweetener*

FRUIT SALAD

- *225 g/8 oz strawberries, hulled and halved* ● *100 g/4 oz seedless grapes*
- *4 kiwi fruit, peeled, halved and sliced*
- *4 peaches, peeled (see page 13), halved, stoned and cut in cubes*

1 Place the flour and salt in a bowl, then mix in the yeast. Heat the milk until just hand hot. Make a well in the flour, then pour in the milk. Beat the eggs and add them to the milk with the butter. Gradually beat in the flour to make a smooth batter. Carry on beating the batter hard until it develops an elastic texture – this takes about 5 minutes or slightly longer.

2 Thoroughly grease a deep 23 cm/9 in ring tin.

3 Pour the batter into the tin and cover it loosely with oiled polythene, then leave in a warm place until the batter is risen to the top of the tin – this can take several hours, depending on the room temperature.

4 Set the oven at 200°C, 400°F, gas 6.

5 Bake the savarin for 35–40 minutes, until golden and firm. Leave to cool for 2 minutes in the tin, then turn it out on a wire rack to cool completely.

6 Mix the rum, water and sweetener. Place the savarin on a serving platter or stand, and prick it all over with a skewer. Carefully spoon the rum mixture over the savarin, trickling it slowly so that it soaks in.

7 Mix the fruit for the salad, then pile it up in the middle of the ring. If there is any fruit salad left over serve it separately with individual portions.

8 Serve with whipped cream or fromage frais.

SAVARIN IDEAS

Vary the fruit salad according to whatever is in season. Instead of rum, the savarin may be soaked in sweetened fruit juice – orange or pineapple are particularly successful. Heat the juice and spoon it over the hot savarin, then fill the middle with stewed fruit and serve with steaming hot custard.

RUM BABAS

Make a half quantity of the yeast batter and add 3 tbsp sultanas. Divide between 8 well-greased individual ring tins or ramekin dishes. When risen, bake at 220°C, 425°F, gas 7 for 15 minutes. Soak with the rum mixture and serve with whipped cream.

PLUM AND BANANA SAVARIN

Poach 450 g/1 lb halved and stoned plums with 1–2 tbsp water sprinkled over until just tender. Stir in 2 large, sliced bananas and ladle the mixture into the middle of the hot savarin soaked in rum. Serve at once.

BREADS, CAKES AND BISCUITS

This, I am sorry to admit, is where the lack of sugar can be limiting but, on the positive side, there are healthy and tasty alternatives to traditional baking.

Traditional scones, breads and tea-breads are not a problem at all since they do not need sugar either for success in the making or for good eating. A few sultanas or other dried fruit in scones, buns or bread provide quite adequate sweetening.

The down side of baking without sugar is that the results do not keep well. Sugar is a preserving agent, so without it the baked goods tend to become mouldy and inedible after a couple of days. Storing cakes in an airtight polythene bag in the refrigerator (middle or towards the top) means they keep longer but the best idea is to slice and freeze cakes, then individual portions may be quickly thawed as required.

BOILED FRUIT CAKE

MAKES **12** SLICES

This is a semi-rich fruit cake which serves very well for celebrations such as Christmas or significant birthdays. Although it does not need maturing, it keeps well for 2–3 weeks but should not be stored for long periods. If you want to prepare it in advance, then plan to freeze it.

FOOD VALUES	CARBOHYDRATE	FIBRE	FAT	KCALS/KJ
TOTAL	350G	41G	158G	4076/17162
PER SLICE	29G	3G	13G	340/1430

- *225 g/8 oz sultanas* • *225 g/8 oz raisins* • *225 g/8 oz currants*
- *grated rind and juice of 1 orange* • *250 ml/8 fl oz freshly brewed tea*
- *225 g/8 oz self-raising wholemeal flour* • *100 g/4 oz butter or margarine*
- *100 g/4 oz ground almonds* • *2 tsp ground mixed spice* • *2 eggs*

1 Place all the fruit in a saucepan with the orange rind and juice. Pour in the tea and put over medium heat until the liquid boils. Stir well and simmer for 5 minutes, uncovered, then stir again, cover and leave to cool.

2 Line and grease a 20-cm/8-in round deep cake tin.

3 Set the oven at 160°C, 325°F, gas 3.

4 Place the flour in a bowl and rub in the butter or margarine. Stir in the almonds and spice. Make a well in the middle of the dry ingredients, then tip in all the fruit and its juice, and add the eggs. Stir all the ingredients together until thoroughly combined.

5 Turn the mixture into the tin and spread it out evenly. Bake for 2 hours, cover loosely with foil and continue to cook for a further 30 minutes, or until a skewer inserted into the middle comes out clean of mixture. Leave to cool in the tin for 30 minutes, then turn the cake out on to a wire rack to cool completely.

6 Store in an airtight polythene bag.

SANDWICH CAKE

MAKES **10** SLICES

Without a large quantity of sugar it is not possible to make a really light, fluffy, creamed sandwich cake – there are recipes that suggest small amounts of sugar but the results are usually depressingly poor. This alternative method makes a cake which is soft, close-textured and pleasing when sandwiched with a fruit spread. Do not be put off by the crusty appearance as the surface softens on cooling. The lemon rind really lifts this cake – it may not be a classic Victoria sandwich but it's a jolly good sugar-free layer cake!

FOOD VALUES	CARBOHYDRATE	FIBRE	FAT	KCALS/KJ
TOTAL (WITH APRICOT SP) (WITH CHOCOLATE SP)	297G 288G	13G 11G	403G 430G	2353/9861 2629/10983
PER PORTION (WITH APRICOT SP) (WITH CHOCOLATE SP)	30G 29G	1G 1G	40G 43G	235/986 263/1098

- 350 g/12 oz plain flour ● 1 tsp bicarbonate of soda
- 100 g/4 oz margarine ● 12 tbsp sweetener
- 2 tsp natural vanilla essence ● grated rind and juice of 1 lemon
- 3 eggs, beaten ● 200 ml/7 fl oz milk
- 6 tbsp Apricot Spread (page 68) or Chocolate Spread (page 69)

1 Line the bases and grease two 18 cm/7 in sandwich tins.

2 Set the oven at 180°C, 350°F, gas 4.

3 Mix the flour and bicarbonate of soda, then rub in the margarine and stir in the sweetener. Add the vanilla, lemon rind and juice, eggs and milk and beat well until thoroughly combined in a thick, smooth batter.

4 Divide the batter between the prepared tins and bake for 35–40 minutes, until well risen, browned and firm to the touch. Turn out to cool on a wire rack.

5 Sandwich the cooled cakes together with Apricot Spread or Chocolate Spread.

JENNI'S MUFFINS

MAKES **24**

A contribution from a fellow food-lover and cook, these American-style muffins baked in deep patty tins are very simple and quite mouthwatering. Serve them freshly baked, with butter as a treat, and fruit spread or munch through them plain.

FOOD VALUES	CARBOHYDRATE	FIBRE	FAT	KCALS/KJ
TOTAL	172.5G	52G	50G	1274/5365
PER MUFFIN	7G	2G	2G	53/224

- 150 g/5 oz wholemeal flour ● 50 g/2 oz bran ● 1 tsp bicarbonate of soda
- pinch of salt ● 100 g/4 oz dried mixed fruit ● 1 egg
- 3 tbsp sunflower oil ● 200 ml/7 fl oz milk

1 Set the oven at 200°C, 400°F, gas 6 and thoroughly grease two trays of deep muffin tins. If you only have a dozen tins, then cook the mixture in two batches – it lasts perfectly well.

2 Mix all the dry ingredients in a bowl, then make a well in the middle. Add the egg, oil and milk. Beat the liquids, then gradually beat in the dry ingredients until thoroughly combined in a thick batter.

3 Drop spoonfuls of mixture into the tins to just fill them. Bake for 10–15 minutes, until well risen, firm to the touch and browned. Cool on a wire rack and serve warm.

VARIATIONS

APRICOT NUT MUFFINS

Add 225 g/8 oz chopped ready-to-eat dried apricots and 50 g/2 oz chopped walnuts instead of the dried fruit.

FIG AND ALMOND MUFFINS

Finely chop 100 g/4 oz dried figs and 100 g/4 oz blanched almonds. Add to the mixture with the grated rind of 1 orange. Omit the mixed dried fruit.

RAISIN MUFFINS

Use raisins instead of the dried fruit.

APPLE MUESLIES

MAKES 12 SQUARES

If you do not have home-made muesli, then use an unsweetened commercial version which does not have any added milk powder.

FOOD VALUES	CARBOHYDRATE	FIBRE	FAT	KCALS/KJ
TOTAL	280G	33G	49G	1645/6943
PER SQUARE	23G	3G	4G	137/579

- *350 g/12 oz dessert apples, peeled, cored and chopped*
- *4 tbsp fresh orange juice* • *25 g/1 oz margarine*
- *350 g/12 oz Home-made Muesli (page 9)*

1 Set the oven at 190°C, 375°F, gas 5.

2 Line the base and grease a 25 x 18 cm/10 x 7 in shallow tin.

3 Place the apples and orange juice in a saucepan and heat until the juice is boiling. Reduce the heat, cover the pan tightly and cook, stirring occasionally, for 15 minutes, or until the apples are tender. They do not have to be cooked down to a smooth sauce.

4 Beat the margarine into the apples, then stir in the muesli. Mix well so that the muesli and apples are evenly combined, then turn the mixture into the tin and press it down well. Bake for 45–50 minutes, until firm and well browned on top.

5 Leave the mixture to cool for 30 minutes, then cut it into twelve squares and set aside to cool completely. Remove the cold apple mueslies from the tin – the first one usually breaks as it is lifted out but careful use of a palette knife ensures that the others come out in good shape.

APPLE AND CARROT CAKE

MAKES 16 SLICES

This is moist, well flavoured and very successful.

FOOD VALUES	CARBOHYDRATE	FIBRE	FAT	KCALS/KJ
TOTAL	255G	32G	169G	2729/11400
PER PER SLICE	16G	2G	11G	171/713

- *225 g/8 oz self-raising wholemeal flour* • *100 g/4 oz margarine*
- *1 tsp cinnamon* • *100 g/4 oz walnuts, chopped* • *100 g/4 oz raisins*
- *225 g/8 oz dessert apples, peeled, cored and grated*
- *100 g/4 oz carrot, grated* • *grated rind of 1 orange*
- *2 large eggs* • *4 tbsp fresh orange juice*

1 Line the base and grease a 900 g/2 lb loaf tin.

2 Set the oven at 180°C, 350°F, gas 4.

3 Place the flour in a bowl and mix well, then rub in the margarine and stir in the cinnamon. Stir in the walnuts, raisins, apples and carrot. Add the orange rind, eggs and juice, then beat well until thoroughly combined.

4 Spoon the mixture into the prepared tin, smooth the top and bake for about 1¼ hours, or until the cake is well-risen and firm to the touch. Turn out and cool on a wire rack.

EASY PINWHEEL BUNS

MAKES **9**

These are a useful cook's cheat, making use of bread mix instead of weighing and preparing a traditional dough. If you need the extra fibre to balance the content of other meals, you can use a wholemeal bread mix, but the results are not so pleasing.

FOOD VALUES	CARBOHYDRATE	FIBRE	FAT	KCALS/KJ
TOTAL	355G	12G	10G	1565/6401
PER BUN	39G	1G	1G	174/711

- *175 g/6 oz mixed dried fruit* ● *150 ml/¼ pt unsweetened apple juice*
- *283 g/10 oz packet white bread mix* ● *200 ml/7 fl oz milk, warmed*
- *a little flour* ● *1 tsp ground cinnamon*

1 Place the fruit in a saucepan with the apple juice and bring to the boil. Reduce the heat and simmer for 10 minutes, or until the juice has evaporated, shaking the pan frequently towards the end of cooking to avoid burning. Set aside to cool slightly.

2 Grease a 23-cm/9-in square tin.

3 Make up the bread mix following the packet instructions, using the milk instead of water. Knead the dough until smooth and elastic, then roll it out on a lightly floured surface into a 23–25 cm/9–10 in square.

4 Mix the cinnamon into the fruit, then spread it over the dough, leaving a clear gap all around the edge. Dampen the edges of the dough. Roll up the dough from one side, like a Swiss roll.

5 Use a sharp knife to cut the roll into nine even slices, then place these cut sides up in the greased tin. Cover loosely with oiled polythene and leave in a warm place until well risen – the dough should be doubled in thickness and this will take some considerable time.

6 Meanwhile, set the oven at 220°C, 425°F, gas 7.

7 Bake the rolls for 20–30 minutes, until browned and firm. Allow to cool in the baking tin for 15 minutes, then transfer them to a wire rack.

8 The pinwheels are delicious served warm.

OATCAKES

MAKES 12

FOOD VALUES	CARBOHYDRATE	FIBRE	FAT	KCALS/KJ
TOTAL	162.5G	16G	39G	1083/4560
PER OATCAKE	13.5G	1G	3G	90/380

- *175 g/6 oz medium oatmeal* • *50 g/2 oz wholemeal flour*
- *½ tsp bicarbonate of soda* • *½ tsp salt* • *50 ml/2 fl oz milk*
- *2 tbsp sunflower oil*

1 Set the oven at 180°C, 350°F, gas 4.

2 Grease a baking tray.

3 Mix the oatmeal, flour, bicarbonate of soda and salt in a bowl and make a well in the middle.

4 Pour in the milk and oil, then gradually mix in the dry ingredients to make a stiff dough. Turn the dough out on to a lightly floured surface and knead it briefly until smooth. Cut the dough in half, then cut each half into six equal portions.

5 Pat or roll out each portion of dough into a biscuit measuring about 10 cm/4 in in diameter. Place the biscuits on the prepared tray and bake them for 15 minutes, until firm and lightly browned. Leave on the tray for 2 minutes, then transfer the oatcakes to a wire rack to cool.

VARIATIONS

Instead of patting out individual biscuits, halve the dough and roll it into two 18–20 cm/7–8 in circles. Place on greased baking trays and cut each round into 6 wedges. Do not separate the wedges. Bake as in the main recipe.

PARMESAN CRACKERS

Add 4 tbsp grated Parmesan cheese and 2 tbsp snipped chives to the mixture.

HERB OATCAKES

Add 1 tsp dried mixed herbs.

ONION OATCAKES

Finely chop 1 onion and add it to the mixture together with the oil and the milk.

PRUNE AND NUT TEA-BREAD

MAKES 10 SLICES

Other dried fruit may be used in place of prunes – raisins or sultanas are good, or simply add a little mixed dried fruit.

FOOD VALUES	CARBOHYDRATE	FIBRE	FAT	KCALS/KJ
TOTAL	178.5G	26G	62G	1399/5874
PER SLICE	18G	3G	6G	140/587

- *225 g/8 oz strong wholemeal flour* • *½ tsp salt* • *25 g/1 oz margarine*
- *75 g/3 oz ready-to-eat prunes, stoned and roughly chopped*
- *50 g/2 oz walnuts, finely chopped* • *1 sachet easy-blend dried yeast*
- *150 ml/¼ pt milk*

1 Place the flour in a bowl and add the salt. Rub in the margarine, then stir in the yeast, prunes and walnuts. Heat the milk until it is hand hot – if it gets any hotter, leave it to cool before adding it to the yeast mixture.

2 Make a well in the dry ingredients, then add the milk and gradually mix it into the ingredients to make a firm dough. Add an extra few drops of milk if necessary to bind the ingredients but do not make the dough sticky.

3 Grease a 450-g/1-lb bread tin. Turn the dough out on a lightly floured surface and knead it thoroughly for 10 minutes, until smooth and elastic. Press stray nuts back into the dough as you knead it. Place the dough in the tin, pressing it down into the corners. Cover the top loosely with oiled polythene and leave the tea-bread in a warm place until risen in a dome above the rim of the tin – this can take up to a couple of hours depending on the heat of the dough and the room.

4 Set the oven at 220°C, 425°F, gas 7.

5 Brush the loaf with a little warm water, then bake it for 35–40 minutes, until browned on top. Turn the loaf out and tap its base – it should produce a hollow sound when the bread is cooked. Cool on a wire rack.

6 Serve sliced and spread thinly with butter, margarine or low-fat spread.

FRUIT AND NUT CAKE

MAKES **8** SLICES

Make a small one because a large cake will not keep unless frozen.

FOOD VALUES	CARBOHYDRATE	FIBRE	FAT	KCALS/KJ
TOTAL	250G	19G	149G	2394/9996
PER SLICE	31G	2G	19G	299/1250

- *75 g/3 oz self-raising flour* ● *100 g/4 oz self-raising wholemeal flour*
- *75 g/3 oz margarine* ● *175 g/6 oz dried mixed fruit*
- *100 g/4 oz walnuts or hazelnuts, chopped* ● *2 eggs, beaten*
- *4 tbsp unsweetened apple juice*

1 Base line and grease an 15-cm/6-in round deep cake tin.

2 Set the oven at 180°C, 350°F, gas 4.

3 Mix both flours, then rub in the margarine. Stir in the fruit and nuts, followed by the eggs and apple juice to bind the ingredients in a soft mixture.

4 Spoon the mixture into the tin and spread it out evenly, then bake for 1–1¼ hours, until risen, browned and firm to the touch. A skewer inserted into the middle of the cake should come out clean of mixture. Cool the cake on a wire rack.

CHOCOLATE DATE LOAF

MAKES **16** SLICES

Now this is successful! Take note of the quantity of dates, though, as they naturally have a high sugar content. By the way, use the block cooking-dates, not the ready-chopped fruit that is rolled in sugar, and chop them finely – a food processor is ideal or use a large, sharp cook's knife.

FOOD VALUES	CARBOHYDRATE	FIBRE	FAT	KCALS/KJ
TOTAL	306G	28G	118G	2473/10381
PER SLICE	19G	2G	7G	155/649

- *225 g/8 oz self-raising wholemeal flour* ● *100 g/4 oz margarine*
- *3 tbsp cocoa powder* ● *6 tbsp sweetener*
- *225 g/8 oz cooking-dates, finely chopped* ● *3 large eggs, beaten*
- *3 tbsp milk*

1 Line the base and grease a 900 g/2 lb loaf tin.

2 Set the oven at 180°C, 350°F, gas 4.

3 Put the flour in a bowl, then rub in the margarine. Stir in the cocoa, sweetener and dates. Add the eggs and milk and mix until thoroughly combined.

4 Spoon the mixture into the tin, smooth the top and bake for about 1¼ hours, until well risen and firm to the touch. Turn out to cool on a wire rack.

SCONES

MAKES **8**

Good home-made scones are a real tea-time treat, ten times better than a gooey cake in my opinion! Transform them into a perfectly acceptable "cream" tea by serving them with one of the fruit spreads in the following chapter and a dish of curd cheese softened with low-fat fromage frais. Of course, there is no reason to avoid dolloping on some clotted cream as a real summertime treat and adding a few fresh strawberries into the bargain – but avoid the cream on a frequent basis. I use cream of tartar and bicarbonate of soda to make light, well risen scones – you can always opt to use 3 tsp baking-powder instead but, in my opinion, the result is not quite as good! By the way, a common mistake is to roll out the dough too thinly, resulting in scones that are miserably shallow.

1 Set the oven at 220°C, 425°F, gas 7.

2 Grease a baking tray.

3 Mix the flours, cream of tartar and bicarbonate of soda, then rub in the butter or margarine and stir in the sultanas if used. Mix in enough milk to make a soft, but not sticky, dough.

4 Turn the dough out on a lightly floured surface and knead very briefly until just smooth. Roll out to 1.5 cm/¾ in thick (or slightly thicker) and stamp out 6 cm/2½ in round scones.

5 Place on the baking tray, brush with a little milk and bake for about 10 minutes. Cool on a wire rack.

FOOD VALUES	CARBOHYDRATE	FIBRE	FAT	KCALS/KJ
TOTAL	200G	13G	46G	1299/5396
PER SCONE	25G	2G	6G	162/675

- 100 g/4 oz plain flour ● 100 g/4 oz wholemeal flour
- 2 tsp cream of tartar ● 1 tsp bicarbonate of soda
- 50 g/2 oz butter or margarine ● 75 g/3 oz sultanas (optional)
- 100 ml/4 fl oz milk

OATY BISCUITS

MAKES **12**

FOOD VALUES	CARBOHYDRATE	FIBRE	FAT	KCALS/KJ
TOTAL	14.2G	13G	55G	1100/4615
PER BISCUIT	1.2G	1G	5G	92/385

● *50 g/2 oz wholemeal flour* ● *½ tsp bicarbonate of soda*
● *100 g/4 oz rolled oats* ● *grated rind and juice of 1 orange*
● *50 g/2 oz sultanas* ● *4 tbsp oil* ● *3 tbsp unsweetened apple juice*

1 Set the oven at 180°C, 350°F, gas 4 and grease a baking tray.

2 Mix the flour, bicarbonate of soda, oats, orange rind and sultanas. Mix in the oil and orange juice with enough apple juice to make a firm dough.

3 Turn the dough out on to a floured surface and knead it lightly, then divide it in half and cut each half into six equal portions. Flatten each portion into a 6–7.5 cm/2½–3 in circle.

4 Place the biscuits on the tray as they are shaped and bake for 15–20 minutes, until browned. Transfer the biscuits to a wire rack in order to cool.

SIMPLE BISCUITS

MAKES **14**

FOOD VALUES	CARBOHYDRATE	FIBRE	FAT	KCALS/KJ
TOTAL	74G	6G	42.5G	722/2590
PER BISCUIT	5G	0.5G	3G	52/211

● *50 g/2 oz plain flour* ● *50 g/2 oz wholemeal flour*
● *½ tsp bicarbonate of soda* ● *50 g/2 oz butter or margarine*
● *4 tbsp sweetener* ● *2 tbsp unsweetened apple juice*

1 Set the oven at 180°C, 350°F, gas 4.

2 Grease a baking tray. Mix both types of flour with the bicarbonate of soda, then rub in the butter or margarine and stir in the artificial sweetener and apple juice to bind the dough.

3 Divide the dough in half. Keep one portion wrapped in polythene while you roll and cut out the other piece of dough. Roll the dough out thinly and stamp out 6 cm/2½ in round biscuits. Re-roll trimmings and stamp out more biscuits. Repeat with the second portion of dough.

4 Place the biscuits on the baking tray and bake for 10–15 minutes. Cool on the tray for a minute, then transfer to a wire rack.

VARIATIONS

VANILLA BISCUITS

Add 1 tsp natural vanilla flavouring to the mixture at the same time as the apple juice.

ORANGE BISCUITS

Add the grated rind of 1 orange.

HAZELNUT FRUIT BISCUITS

Add 4 tbsp chopped toasted hazelnuts and 3 tbsp chopped raisins to the dry ingredients.

CHOCOLATE SANDWICH BISCUITS

Add 1 tbsp cocoa powder to the dry ingredients. Sandwich the biscuits in pairs with Chocolate Spread (page 69).

ALMOND CREAMS

Add 1 tsp oil of bitter almonds and 4 tbsp ground almonds to the mixture. Sandwich the cooked biscuits together with frangipane cream (see Frangipane Fruit Tart, page 49).

CUSTARD SANDWICH BISCUITS

Add 1 tsp natural vanilla flavouring to the mixture with the juice. Sandwich the cooled biscuits together with Confectioner's Custard (see Apple and Orange Trifle, page 50) just before eating.

ALTERNATIVE PRESERVES

I hesitate to use the term preserves in this chapter title because without sugar the recipes do not have excellent keeping qualities. However, here are a few recipes that taste good, that work well and do not contain added sugar. The vinegar content of the chutneys and savoury pickles makes them suitable for long storage but they may not compare with traditional recipes containing sugar. Remember to date the jars and if there is any sign of mould when a preserve is opened, then discard it. Once opened the chutneys should be stored in the refrigerator.

I have included a selection of fruit spreads made without sugar and thickened with agar-agar. Agar-agar sets at a higher temperature than gelatine and gives my mock jams a better result.

The best way to store the fruit spreads is to freeze them in small portions which you can thaw and use within 3–4 days. Keep them covered in the refrigerator once thawed. They can also be stored for long periods by processing as for bottled fruit: if you intend doing this consult an authoritative source.

MARROW CHUTNEY

MAKES 1.8 KG/4 LB

The combination of apples and raisins sweetens this chutney sufficiently to give a tangy preserve. Sweetener may be added at the end of cooking for a sweet-sour chutney.

FOOD VALUES	CARBOHYDRATE	FIBRE	FAT	KCALS/KJ
TOTAL	246G	20G	4G	1013/4292
PER 15 ML/1 TBSP	4G	0.5G	TRACE	17/72

- 675 g/1½ lb marrow, seeded and peeled ● 450 g/1 lb onions
- 350 g/12 oz dessert apples, peeled and cored ● 225 g/8 oz raisins
- 2 tsp ground ginger ● ½ tsp turmeric ● 300 ml/½ pt cider vinegar

1 Roughly chop the marrow and place it in a large saucepan. Mince or finely chop the onions, apples and raisins, then add them to the pan. Stir in the ginger, turmeric and vinegar.

2 Bring the chutney to the boil, stirring, then reduce the heat and simmer for about 1½ hours, stirring occasionally, until reduced and thickened. Stir more frequently towards the end of cooking to prevent the mixture sticking to the pan.

3 Prepare warm, thoroughly clean pots and transfer the chutney to them immediately it is cooked. Top at once with discs of waxed paper and airtight lids. Label and store in a cool, dry place. Allow to mature for 2 weeks before use.

BEETROOT CHUTNEY

MAKES **2.8 KG/6 LB**

This is very successful – the sort of chutney that tastes good as a filling for baked potatoes, sprinkled with some grated cheese, or spooned over low-fat soft cheese. It makes delicious sandwiches with low-fat soft cheese.

FOOD VALUES	CARBOHYDRATE	FIBRE	FAT	KCALS/KJ
TOTAL	186G	38G	3G	1352/5746
PER 15 ML/1 TBSP	2G	0.5G	TRACE	15/62

- 1 kg/2¼ lb raw beetroot ● 450 g/1 lb dessert apples, peeled and cored
- 450 g/1 lb onions, chopped ● 225 g/8 oz sultanas
- 1 garlic clove, crushed (optional) ● 2 tsp ground allspice
- ¼ tsp chilli powder ● ½ tsp salt ● 750 ml/1¼ pt cider vinegar
- 6 tbsp sweetener

1 Peel the beetroot, then coarsely grate it and place it in a saucepan. Grate or chop the apples and add them to the pan with the onions. Chop the sultanas and add them to the pan – chopping the sultanas is not essential but it does give a better chutney in terms of sweetness.

2 Add the garlic, allspice, chilli powder, salt and vinegar. Bring to the boil, stirring, then reduce the heat and cover the pan. Simmer for 1 hour, stirring occasionally. Remove the lid and simmer for a further 30 minutes, until the chutney is thickened. Remove from the heat and stir in the sweetener.

3 Prepare warm, clean jars and pot the chutney as soon as it is cooked. Cover with waxed discs and airtight lids at once. Store in a cool place, free from damp, and allow to mature for at least a week before eating.

PICCALILLI

MAKES **1 KG/2 LB**

This is very successful – the sweetener works well to balance the cider vinegar.

FOOD VALUES	CARBOHYDRATE	FIBRE	FAT	KCALS/KJ
TOTAL	120G	21G	12G	651/2731
PER 15 ML/1 TBSP	4G	0.5G	0.5G	20/82

- 225 g/8 oz carrots, trimmed, peeled and diced
- 4 celery sticks, diced ● 450 g/1 lb onions, chopped
- 450 g/1 lb cauliflower florets ● 450 g/1 lb cucumber, peeled and diced
- 4 tbsp salt ● 450 ml/¾ pt cider vinegar ● 2 tbsp plain flour
- 1 tbsp English mustard powder ● 1 tsp turmeric ● ½ tsp ground ginger
- 8 tbsp sweetener

1 Place all the vegetables in a bowl, sprinkling a little salt over each layer. Cover and leave to stand overnight. Next day, drain well, and rinse the vegetables very quickly under cold water, then drain again.

2 Place the vegetables in a saucepan and add three-quarters of the vinegar. Bring to the boil, then reduce the heat and cover the pan. Simmer for 5 minutes.

3 Blend the flour, mustard, turmeric and ginger to a paste with the remaining vinegar. Add some of the hot liquid to the paste, stirring all the time, until it is well thinned. Turn the heat off under the pickle, then pour in the paste, stirring all the time to prevent lumps forming.

4 Bring to the boil, stirring, reduce the heat, cover and cook gently for 10 minutes. Stir in the sweetener and pot the pickle at once. Cover with discs of waxed paper, wax down, and airtight lids. Allow to mature for 1 week before using. Store in a cool, dry place.

APPLE AND APRICOT CHUTNEY

MAKES **1.8 KG/4 LB**

This is a simple chutney, none the worse for not having large quantities of sugar added. It is important to use cider vinegar as it is significantly less harsh than either malt or wine vinegars. Although the concentrated, cooked fruit and fruit juice is naturally high in sugar, chutney is usually eaten in small amounts.

FOOD VALUES	CARBOHYDRATE	FIBRE	FAT	KCALS/KJ
TOTAL	327G	49G	6G	1395/5881
PER 15 ML/1 TBSP	7G	1G	TRACE	30/126

• 450 ml/¾ pt unsweetened apple juice • 1.4 kg/3 lb cooking-apples
• 1.4 kg/3 lb onions • 1 garlic clove, crushed • 2 tsp ground cinnamon
• 2 tsp ground coriander • ½ tsp ground cloves
• 600 ml/1 pt cider vinegar
• 225 g/8 oz ready-to-eat dried apricots, chopped • 6 tbsp sweetener

1 Pour the apple juice into a large saucepan – use stainless steel or a good non-stick pan but avoid copper, aluminium or any uncoated metal. Bring to the boil, then boil for about 5 minutes, or until reduced by half.

2 Peel, core and mince or chop the apples. Peel and mince or chop the onions. A food processor or liquidizer may be used for this, the former being ideal. Add the apples and onions to the reduced apple juice, then stir in the spices and pour in the vinegar. Stir in the apricots.

3 Bring to the boil, stirring, then reduce the heat and simmer gently, uncovered, until thick – about 1½–2 hours. Stir occasionally during cooking to prevent the chutney sticking to the bottom of the pan. This is particularly important towards the end of the cooking time. Off the heat, stir in the artificial sweetener.

4 Have clean, warm jars ready and pot the chutney as soon as it is cooked. Cover immediately with discs of waxed paper (waxed side down) and airtight lids. Label and store in a cool, dry place. Allow it to mature for a couple of weeks before eating.

UNSWEETENED MINCEMEAT

MAKES **1.4KG/3 LB**

This is made without suet, keeping the fat content low and making it useful for vegetarians as well. Make this 1–3 weeks in advance, or freeze it if you intend keeping it for longer.

FOOD VALUES	CARBOHYDRATE	FIBRE	FAT	KCALS/KJ
TOTAL	326G	41G	135G	3877/16308
PER 15 ML/1 TBSP	3.5G	0.5G	1.5G	42/174

- *450 g/1 lb cooking-apples, peeled, cored and minced or grated*
- *225 g/8 oz carrots, trimmed, peeled and grated*
- *225 g/8 oz sultanas, minced or chopped*
- *225 g/8 oz raisins, minced or chopped*
- *225 g/8 oz currants, minced or chopped*
- *100 g/4 oz cut mixed peel, minced or chopped fine*
- *225 g/8 oz blanched almonds, chopped*
- *grated rind and juice of 2 oranges* • *1 tsp cinnamon*
- *1 tsp grated nutmeg* • *¼ tsp ground cloves* • *6 tbsp brandy or rum*

1 Place all the ingredients in a large bowl and mix well. Leave to stand for 10 hours, stirring as often as possible to mix the fruits with the juices, spices and brandy.

2 Immerse pots and their airtight lids in a pan of water and bring very slowly to the boil over low to medium heat. Put the lids in the pan separately from the pots and do not put over high heat in case the jars break. Boil for 5 minutes, then drain well and allow to dry upside-down on a clean folded tea-towel.

3 Pot the mincemeat in the jars, pressing it down well, and cover at once. Store in the refrigerator. Alternatively, pack in freezer containers and freeze. Do not keep the mincemeat for longer than 3 weeks in the refrigerator. However, it may be frozen for up to a year.

APRICOT SPREAD

MAKES **1.4L/2¼ PT**

Use ordinary dried apricots for this rather than the ready-to-eat type. If the local supermarket does not have them, try the whole-food shop – traditional dried apricots that need soaking are cheaper than the other type.

FOOD VALUES	CARBOHYDRATE	FIBRE	FAT	KCALS/KJ
TOTAL	208G	36G	3.5G	890/3776
PER 15 ML/1 TBSP	2G	0.5G	TRACE	10/40

- *450 g/1 lb dried apricots* • *1 cinnamon stick*
- *675 g/1½ lb cooking-apples, peeled, cored and chopped*
- *grated rind and juice of 1 lemon* • *1½ tsp agar-agar*
- *6–8 tbsp sweetener*

1 Place the apricots in a bowl and pour in cold water to cover them by 2.5 cm/1 in. Cover and leave to stand overnight.

2 Tip the soaked apricots and their juice into a saucepan. Add the cinnamon, apples, lemon rind and juice. Bring to the boil, stirring, then reduce the heat and cover the pan. Simmer the fruit for 1 hour, stirring occasionally.

3 Uncover the pan and remove the cinnamon stick, then sprinkle in the agar-agar and stir well. Cook for a minute or so, until the mixture bubbles and the agar-agar has dissolved completely.

4 Off the heat, stir in the sweetener, then cool completely. Transfer to small containers and pack in a polythene bag, then label and freeze. The spread will keep in a covered container in the refrigerator for up to a week.

LEMON SPREAD

MAKES **900 ML/1 ½ PT**

FOOD VALUES	CARBOHYDRATE	FIBRE	FAT	KCALS/KJ
TOTAL	81G	12G	1G	322/1361
PER 15 ML/1 TBSP	1G	TRACE	TRACE	5/23

- *3 lemons* • *675 g/1½ lb dessert apples* • *2 tsp agar-agar*
- *6–8 tbsp sweetener*

1 Thinly peel the lemons, cutting off just the rind. Cut the rind into thin shreds, then place them in a saucepan. Halve the lemons and squeeze their juice, then make it up to 600 ml/1 pt with water. Bring to the boil, reduce the heat and cover the pan. Simmer for 1 hour.

2 Peel, core and chop the apples, then add them to the pan. Bring to the boil, reduce the heat so the mixture simmers steadily and cover the pan. Cook for 20 minutes.

3 Sprinkle the agar-agar over the fruit, then stir well for a further minute or so, until the setting agent has completely dissolved and is thoroughly mixed. The mixture should come back to a simmer, then remove it from the heat. Unlike gelatine, agar-agar is not prevented from setting by reaching boiling point – in fact, the liquid should be boiling to dissolve it.

4 Stir in the sweetener and allow the fruit to cool. Pack in small containers and place in a polythene bag, then seal and freeze. The spread may be stored in a covered container in the refrigerator for up to a week.

CHOCOLATE SPREAD

MAKES **225 G/8 OZ**

This works very well but it is important to avoid sweeteners containing saccharine as they make the spread very bitter.

FOOD VALUES	CARBOHYDRATE	FIBRE	FAT	KCALS/KJ
TOTAL	10.5G	0	66G	840/3401
PER 15 ML/1 TBSP	1G	0	4G	56/227

- *50 g/2 oz unsalted butter* • *3 tbsp cocoa powder*
- *175 g/6 oz low-fat soft cheese (Light Philadelphia or Shape type)*
- *4–6 tbsp sweetener*

1 Melt the butter in a small saucepan. Add the cocoa and cook, stirring, for 3 minutes over low heat. Remove from the heat and leave to cool for 5 minutes.

2 Stir the cheese into the cocoa, then mix in the sweetener to taste. Chill the chocolate spread in a covered container and it will keep for about 3–5 days in the refrigerator, depending on the shelf-life of the cheese.

STRAWBERRY TOPPER

MAKES **750 ML/ABOUT 1¼ PT**

This is a topping good spread for bread-and-butter, scones, or cakes that are going to be eaten up quickly!

FOOD VALUES	CARBOHYDRATE	FIBRE	FAT	KCALS/KJ
TOTAL	63G	15G	1G	286/1190
PER 15 ML/1 TBSP	1G	0.5G	TRACE	6/26

- *450 g/1 lb dessert apples, peeled, cored and grated*
- *juice of 1 lemon* ● *2 tbsp water* ● *450 g/1 lb strawberries, hulled*
- *1 tsp agar-agar* ● *2 tbsp sweetener (optional)*

1 Mix the apples and lemon juice in a saucepan, adding 2 tbsp water. Heat gently until the small amount of liquid is boiling, then put the lid on the pan and cook for 15 minutes, stirring once, until the apples are soft.

2 Add the strawberries, mix well, then re-cover the pan and continue cooking for 30 minutes, stirring occasionally, until the fruit is soft.

3 Stir the agar-agar into the hot fruit and cook for about a minute, until the mixture bubbles and the agar-agar is dissolved completely. Off the heat, stir in the sweetener, then divide between small freezer containers and allow to cool. Pack in a polythene bag, label and freeze. The spread may be kept in a covered container in the refrigerator for up to 3 days.

ORANGE FREEZER MARMALADE

MAKES **1.4 L/2¼ PT**

This is not to be directly compared with traditional high-sugar marmalade; however, it is a very pleasing spread for toast or used in place of traditional marmalades and jams.

FOOD VALUES	CARBOHYDRATE	FIBRE	FAT	KCALS/KJ
TOTAL	36G	7G	0.5G	155/664
PER 15 ML/1 TBSP	0.5G	TRACE	TRACE	2/7

- *2 large oranges* ● *600 ml/1 pt water* ● *4 tsp agar-agar*
- *6 tbsp sweetener*

1 Scrub the oranges, then peel them thinly and save the peel. Cut off all the pith and halve the fruit. Discard the pips, then chop the oranges and the peel. Place the fruit in a saucepan and add the water. Bring to the boil, reduce the heat and cover the pan. Simmer for 1 hour, or until tender.

2 Sprinkle the agar-agar over the fruit and stir thoroughly until it is mixed in. Stir until the fruit bubbles for a minute or so, by which time the agar-agar will have dissolved. Remove from the heat and stir in the sweetener.

3 Transfer the mixture to small, clean freezer containers and allow to cool. Pack in a polythene bag and freeze. The jelly will keep for anything up to 5 days in a covered container on a low shelf in the refrigerator.

CLEVER CONFECTIONERY

Here are a few ideas for alternatives to buying diabetic confectionery, although I have in one case used diabetic chocolate as a coating.

I am pleased with the results and hope you find them useful for times like Christmas, birthdays and other celebrations. They are useful for children to make and good enough for all the family to appreciate the results. They are also significantly less expensive – and in some cases far more healthy – than the commercial alternatives.

ALMOND BITES

MAKES **24**

FOOD VALUES	CARBOHYDRATE	FIBRE	FAT	KCALS/KJ
TOTAL	22G	20G	148G	1657/6864
PER CREAM	1G	1G	6G	69/286

- 225 g/8 oz ground almonds ● 4 tbsp sweetener
- 4 tbsp fromage frais ● ¼ tsp oil of bitter almonds
- 24 blanched almonds, lightly toasted

1 Place the ground almonds in a bowl and mix in the sweetener. Add the fromage frais and almond oil, then gradually mix in the ground almond mixture to make a marzipan-like paste.

2 Press the mixture together with your fingertips, then roll small portions into balls. They should be slightly larger than cherries. Flatten each ball slightly and top with a toasted almond, then place in a paper sweet case. Keep covered and chilled and eat within a week of making.

COOK'S TIP

UNLIKE MARZIPAN . . .

The almond mixture is very like almond paste, only less sweet. It rolls out well, moulds well and is ideal for covering small cakes but, of course, it will not keep in the same way as marzipan in which the sugar acts as a preservative.

ALMOND PINWHEELS

MAKES **21**

FOOD VALUES	CARBOHYDRATE	FIBRE	FAT	KCALS/KJ
TOTAL	12G	10G	75G	844/3497
PER PINWHEEL	1G	0.5G	4G	40/167

- *½ quantity Almond Bites mixture* • *a little cornflour*
- *1 tsp cocoa powder* • *1 tbsp sweetener*

1 Make up the mixture and cut it in half. Lightly dust the surface with cornflour and roll out one piece into a 15-cm/6-in square. Cover with plastic wrap.

2 Knead the cocoa and sweetener into the remaining paste, then roll it out into a 15-cm/6-in square. Lay the cocoa paste on top of the plain paste and roll them both together into an 18-cm/7-in square.

3 Roll up the two-colour paste like a Swiss roll, carefully pressing the paste together if it begins to crack. Cut the dough into slices slightly thicker than 5 mm/¼ in. Give the whole strip a couple of rolls after every one or two slices to keep it in shape, and wipe the knife often.

FRUMBLES

MAKES **30**

A jumble of dried fruits, these frumbles are irresistible but they do contain a lot of dried fruit, so do not overindulge in them.

FOOD VALUES	CARBOHYDRATE	FIBRE	FAT	KCALS/KJ
TOTAL	178G	34G	167G	2358/9828
PER FRUMBLE	6G	1G	6G	79/328

- *175 g/6 oz raisins, chopped*
- *100 g/4 oz ready-to-eat dried apricots, chopped*
- *100 g/4 oz ground almonds* • *100 g/4 oz hazelnuts, chopped and toasted*
- *75 g/3 oz desiccated coconut, lightly toasted*
- *grated rind and juice of ½ orange*

1 Mix the raisins, apricots, almonds, hazelnuts and coconut. Stir in the orange rind and juice to bind the mixture.

2 Press the mixture together well with your hands, then shape it into small balls, slightly larger than cherries and place them in paper sweet cases.

DESSERT MINTS

MAKES **49**

An excellent substitute for expensive commercial dinner mints – but beware, they are very moreish!

FOOD VALUES	CARBOHYDRATE	FIBRE	FAT	KCALS/KJ
TOTAL	122G	0	82G	1324/5531
PER MINT	2.5G	0	2G	27/113

- *225 g/8 oz diabetic chocolate*
- *100 g/4 oz low-fat soft cheese (Light Philadelphia or Shape type)*
- *3 tbsp sweetener* • *peppermint essence*

1 Base-line a 18-cm/7-in square shallow tin with non-stick baking parchment or wax paper. Melt half the chocolate in a basin over hot water, then spread it evenly over the base of the lined tin. Chill until set.

2 Mix the cheese with the sweetener and drops of peppermint essence to taste. Spread this over the chocolate and chill.

3 Melt the remaining chocolate and spread it over the top of the mint mixture. Allow to half set, then use a sharp knife to cut the mixture into 2.5-cm/1-in wide strips. Wipe the knife with a damp cloth after each cut. Turn the tin around and cut the mixture into strips in the opposite direction to make squares. Chill until firm.

4 Turn the mixture out on a sheet of paper or board and peel off the paper. Carefully separate the mint squares. Keep chilled until ready to serve.

COOK'S TIP
ENSURING MINT CONDITION

It is important to use a firm low-fat cheese, not curd cheese or quark which will not set.

Diabetic chocolate separates very easily on heating so do not melt the whole amount in one go. Once the water under the basin is hot enough to soften the chocolate, remove the pan from the heat and stir the chocolate until it melts. If the water gets very hot the chocolate will separate.

TRUFFLES

MAKES **25**

Whether you are making these for diet reasons or not they taste fine. Like the classic truffles made from cream and butter, these are perishable and should be kept chilled. Do not use a saccharine sweetener as the mixture will be very bitter.

FOOD VALUES	CARBOHYDRATE	FIBRE	FAT	KCALS/KJ
TOTAL	14G	3G	153G	1534/6188
PER TRUFFLE	0.5G	TRACE	6G	61/248

- *100 g/4 oz unsalted butter* • *3 tbsp cocoa powder*
- *225 g/8 oz low-fat soft cheese (Light Philadelphia or Shape type)*
- *4 tbsp sweetener* • *2 tbsp rum or brandy*
- *cocoa or desiccated coconut for coating*

1 Heat the butter in a small saucepan, then add the cocoa and cook on a low heat for 1 minute. Remove from the heat and cool for 5 minutes.

2 Stir in the soft cheese, sweetener and rum or brandy, then chill the mixture for about an hour, until firm enough to shape.

3 Roll teaspoons of the mixture into balls, then coat them in cocoa or desiccated coconut. Place in paper cases and chill until ready to pack or serve.

VARIATIONS

ORANGE TRUFFLES

Add the grated rind of 1 orange and substitute orange juice for the rum or brandy if liked.

ALMOND TRUFFLES

Make the mixture as above, adding ½ tsp oil of bitter almonds. Place a whole blanched almond in the middle of each truffle when moulding into shape.

MOCHA TRUFFLES

Dissolve 2 tsp instant coffee in 1 tbsp boiling water, stir in the rum or brandy, then add to the mixture.

STUFFED APRICOTS

MAKES **14**

FOOD VALUES	CARBOHYDRATE	FIBRE	FAT	KCALS/KJ
TOTAL	131G	26G	30G	860/3629
PER APRICOT	9G	2G	2G	61/259

- *50 g/2 oz ground almonds* • *2 tbsp sweetener*
- *1 tsp grated orange rind* • *1 tbsp orange juice*
- *14 ready-to-eat dried apricots*

1 Mix the ground almonds with the sweetener and orange rind, then stir in the juice to bind the mixture into a paste.

2 Using the point of a small knife, carefully slit each apricot and open it. Roll a small ball of the paste and press it into an apricot, then close the fruit around it. Stuff all the apricots in the same way and arrange them in petits fours cases.

THE DIABETIC DIET – A HEALTHY OUTLOOK

RIGHT Fresh vegetables and cereals are excellent sources of fibre, which slows down the rate at which sugar is absorbed into the blood.

FOOD AND ITS FUNCTIONS

Food is made of a number of components: proteins, fats, vitamins, carbohydrates, minerals, fibre and water. These are essential to ensure that the body grows, works and repairs itself throughout life. A good diet is one in which all the nutrients are balanced to suit the person's needs. Although the general requirements are the same for the majority of the population, everyone is different, so the amount of food depends on the individual's own body functions, age, build and life style.

Food is digested by the body to break it down into the separate nutrients so that they can be absorbed and distributed for use.

Proteins are the body-builders, important for growth and to maintain the body by repairing it during constant use.

Fats are complex substances of different types. They are necessary to maintain the body's own essential stores of fat and they provide energy.

Carbohydrates provide energy.

Minerals and Vitamins are used for many reasons, aiding growth and repair, and ensuring the smooth running of the body's normal functions.

Fibre is a form of carbohydrate but it is not a nutrient as such even though it is essential to the efficient functioning of the body. Fibre is the term used for indigestible matter that makes up the structure of plant cells (cellulose) – it is not absorbed but it keeps the process of digestion working easily.

In certain circumstances nutrients can be put to different uses, although this is not always desirable. For example, fat can be broken down to provide energy if there is insufficient carbohydrate available to meet the body's needs. In extreme circumstances protein can also be broken down to provide energy.

UNDERSTANDING CARBOHYDRATES

These can be divided into sugars, starch and cellulose or similar related indigestible material (fibre). Both starch (complex carbohydrate) and sugar eventually yield sugars suitable for use in the body and the speed with which the food is broken down into this "simple" sugar is important. The body's sugar levels rise more quickly by eating sugar than starch, and some types of sugar are absorbed more quickly than others. Similarly, some starch is digested more readily than others and foods rich in fibre are digested more slowly.

There are several different sugars, grouped as simple sugars, or monosaccharides, and disaccharides which have a more complex chemical structure.

SUGARS

Glucose (monosaccharide) – found in fruit and plants, this is the form in which sugar is carried in the body once it has been extracted from the food during digestion.

Fructose (monosaccharide) – found in fruit, honey and some vegetables, this is often termed "fruit sugar".

Galactose (monosaccharide) – although it can be found alone, it is mainly known as a part of lactose.

Sucrose (dissacharide) – from sugar-cane or beet, this is what we think of as "sugar" (white, brown or otherwise). Sucrose is made up of glucose and fructose.

Maltose (dissacharide) – this is the sugar which is formed when starch is broken down, either by digestion or by a chemical process, such as brewing. Maltose is made up of glucose.

Lactose (dissacharide) – this is found in milk. It is made up of glucose and galactose but it is not as sweet as other sugars.

SORBITOL

Sorbitol is a sugar product, manufactured so that it is not absorbed by the body as quickly as glucose or sucrose.

STARCH

Found in plant foods, such as vegetables, cereals and pulses, starch is eventually broken down into sugars when digested.

DIABETES AND DIET

Diabetes Mellitus, to give it its full name, is a condition which affects the absorption of sugar in the body. When carbohydrates are digested, they are carried around in the body in the form of glucose (glucose is found in the blood of living animals). Normally, the body absorbs this sugar to replace the energy which it uses. The amount of sugar in the blood, or the blood sugar level, is controlled in the body by a substance which is released by the pancreas – a hormone known as insulin. Insulin plays a vital role in transferring the sugar from the blood to the body cells where it is used to replace spent energy.

In cases of diabetes, this hormone is not present in sufficient quantities to facilitate the normal use of blood sugar. There are two main types of diabetes: insulin dependent diabetes and non-insulin dependent diabetes.

INSULIN DEPENDENT DIABETES (TYPE 1)

In this case, the pancreas does not produce insulin or it only produces traces of the hormone. This is generally found in young people, although older people may have the condition. Treatment is by injection of insulin and control of diet.

NON-INSULIN DEPENDENT DIABETES (TYPE 2)

This is caused by the slowing down of insulin production – the pancreas does produce some hormone but not enough to meet the needs of the body. This type is common to people in middle age or in older age groups, and it is often related to people who are significantly overweight or have been overweight for some time. Treatment is by diet control, sometimes supplemented by tablets or insulin.

RIGHT Diabetes increases your likelihood of developing atherosclerosis (hardening of the arteries). It is therefore a good idea to keep cholesterol levels in the blood low by avoiding large amounts of saturated animal fats.

BELOW Being a careful shopper is clearly more difficult in an open market, where fresh produce is sold without nutritional information being listed.

GENERAL DIET SENSE

As well as observing specific restrictions related to your carbohydrate intake, it is important to try to maintain a balanced diet which should provide enough energy (calories or kilojoules) to meet your needs. Consume far too many calories and the body will store them in the form of fat; eat slightly too few calories for the amount of energy you expend and your body will break down its own fat reserves and convert them into energy. Your doctor will advise you about your weight and whether you should aim to reduce it. Never put yourself on a reduced-calorie diet without first consulting your doctor or dietitian.

As well as energy in the form of carbohydrate, the food eaten should provide regular supplies of all the nutrients – protein, minerals, vitamins and fats – and fibre which is particularly important in diabetic diet. The majority of the energy supply in the diet should be eaten as complex carbohydrate, with a far smaller proportion coming from fat.

GUIDELINES ON FAT

Fats can be loosely divided into saturated and unsaturated fats. As a general rule animal fats contain more saturated types and fat from vegetable sources is higher in unsaturated forms, although there are exceptions to this and most fats are a mixture of both saturated and unsaturated. The group of unsaturated fats can be further divided into polyunsaturated and monounsaturated.

Recommendations suggest that no more than 35 per cent of the total energy intake (calorie/kilojoule counts) should come from fat. The maximum intake of saturated fat should be no more than 10 per cent and the level of polyunsaturated fat should be in the order of 8 per cent, leaving a suggested figure of 17 per cent for monounsaturated fats.

As well as butter, margarine, oils and spreads, fat is found in milk, cheese, meat, poultry, fish, nuts and seeds. It is most important to adopt a sensible attitude to fat: cutting out butter and obvious animal fats only to replace them with equivalent or large quantities of vegetable fats and oils is not the right approach. Small amounts of animal fats are acceptable; the important point is to reduce overall fat intake by avoiding high-fat convenience foods, fried foods (especially deep fried) and large amounts of high-fat foods. On a daily basis it is advisable to avoid eating significant amounts of fat in foods such as sandwiches (they are quite as good without any fat on the bread), biscuits and snacks.

ALL-IMPORTANT FIBRE

Fibre is important for its function as the waste-disposal train of the body, absorbing water and keeping the contents of the intestine moist as it carries unwanted by-products of digestion out of the body.

In the diabetic diet it plays an essential role in moderating the digestion of food with which it is eaten to slow down the rate by which sugar is absorbed. So, using wholemeal flour and bread, and including fibre in the form of vegetables, whole cereals, beans, lentils, pulses, oats and bran helps to slow down the digestion of starches into sugars, and in the prevention of sudden rises in the sugar levels in the body. Therefore, eat a high proportion of high-fibre foods on a daily basis.

ADAPTING TO A NEW DIET

Always follow the guidelines set down by your doctor or dietitian and go back to them with problems or queries. In many cases, it may not be necessary for strict carbohydrate counts to be given but you will be advised to avoid eating sugar or foods which contain sugar.

Following a sensible diet is neither difficult nor expensive. Pay particular attention to moderating your fat intake.

Eat adequate supplies of protein from lean meat, poultry, fish, beans, pulses, nuts and cereals; plenty of vegetables and fruit (citrus fruit play a helpful role by promoting slow rises in blood sugar levels). Complex carbohydrates and wholegrain ingredients (bread, pasta, rice, pulses and cereals) should play a major part in your meals and cooking but this does not mean that you have to exclude refined grains – the use of white flour, bread, pasta and rice is not taboo!

AVOIDING OR SELECTING SUGARS

Although following a diabetic diet does not necessarily mean excluding all sugar, it does mean that you have to become aware of the foods that contain sugars, the types of sugar and the concentration of sugar naturally occurring in food.

In the past, fructose was considered to be a suitable replacement for sucrose, to be eaten in small, measured amounts given medical approval or by counting it into your carbohydrate allowance. However, current information suggests that limiting the use of sugar to fructose is neither essential nor beneficial, therefore it is suggested that up to a maximum of 25 g/1 oz sucrose per day may be permissible within your carbohydrate allowance.

If you do opt to include sugar, it is important to keep within this maximum and to avoid eating it all at once. It should not be taken in drinks or as a snack but it should be eaten with, or following, a bulk of food, such as for dessert following a meal. If you want to include small amounts of sugar, then check with your doctor, dietitian or clinic first. Remember that you should not include sugar if you are trying to reduce your weight.

SHOPPING

Being an eagle-eyed shopper is, in my opinion, a good practice to follow and when you are diabetic you have to be particularly aware of what you buy. Start by reading labels. Find the ingredients list and look for sugar – not just straightforward "sugar" but any of the forms – honey, syrup, treacle, fructose, maltose, sorbitol and so on. Look for the nutrition information too – if you cannot find it on one brand, then look for another brand of the same or similar food. If your favourite food is not endowed with a note about nutrition, then write to the manufacturer and ask if they can provide you with a consumer's guide to the nutrient content of the food, explaining why you are interested. Check for the carbohydrate, calorie, fat and fibre contents on food labels, the most important being the carbohydrate (and calories if you have to count both).

The best way to find out about food is to set aside time to look around the supermarket when you are not doing your regular shopping. Give yourself an opportunity to wander around looking for foods that are sugar free or contain very little sugar, that have a high fibre content and are low in fat. There are many low-sugar or sugar-free foods, and wholefood shops are a good place to find them. Look for jams and preserves made without added sugar, wholemeal crackers and digestive biscuits.

DIABETIC PRODUCTS

On the whole, these are expensive and unnecessary. Cheaper alternatives are readily found in larger supermarkets or, failing that, in wholefood shops. Check the nutrition information on some diabetic biscuits or similar products as many are comparatively high in fat and they may contain significant quantities of sorbitol or fructose. Diabetic sweets and chocolates are useful occasional "treat" purchases but there are alternatives, as you will see from the closing chapter in this book.

Eating frequent or significant quantities of confectionery, made with added sugars or without them, is not recommended in

any balanced diet and their role in a diabetic diet should be carefully controlled.

ADAPTING FAVOURITE RECIPES

Adapting savoury recipes is not difficult – use low-fat and high-fibre ingredients for everyday cooking as far as possible. If a savoury sauce is sweetened, then add a little sweetener to taste before serving. Sauces that are boiled down with sugar to caramelize them for flavour and colour will not give the same results but remember that boiling to reduce the sauce will concentrate the flavour, even if the texture is not syrupy and the colour not quite so appetizing.

Most desserts and sweet sauces are easily adapted by using sweetener instead of sugar. Aspartame sweeteners do not have a bitter aftertaste, whereas saccharine-based products can produce unpleasant results – particularly with light or bitter ingredients (citrus, cocoa and whipped desserts).

Breads, pastries and scones may be made without sugar, adding some sweetener for cooking if liked. Creamed, whisked and other cakes which rely for success on the chemical changes that take place when sugar is cooked will not work. This book includes a selection of cake recipes, specially created and tested for acceptable results. Reducing the sugar quantity is a solution sometimes offered; however, this is rarely successful.

When making chutneys and sweetened pickles, add an aspartame sweetener after cooking and ensure that the vinegar content is sufficiently high to preserve the ingredients. Jams may be made at home without extra sugar and preserved by a rigid sterilization process as for bottling fruit, or they can be frozen in small packs. Note that preserves without added sugar should be kept refrigerated once opened and used quickly.

EATING OUT

There are two areas of eating out: the first are the occasional treats – a birthday meal, anniversary, weekend jolly, family occasion and so on; the second are the regular meals or snacks – lunch in the canteen, a quick pub lunch away from the office, mid-morning coffee bar snacks are examples of meals eaten away from the home every day or several times a week.

The occasional culinary treat does no harm to even the "healthiest" of diets, so do not feel you have to search a menu for low-fat, high-fibre foods on special occasions. However, it is important to be aware of "hidden" sugar in foods. If in doubt ask – even if the "chef" has not actually cooked the dish he or she may be aware of what they are reheating. Select desserts with caution, opting for fresh fruit and fruit salads in juice; ice-creams can be low in sugar but sorbets and water-ices have a high sugar content and should be avoided. Wholemeal pastry in fruit pies and flans helps to counteract the sugar content by providing bulk which slows down the rate of absorption; however, be wary of custards that are heavily sweetened – a topping of fresh cream will not contain added sugar but crème chantilly will (the cream is whipped with icing sugar).

Regular meals out are slightly different and you should be aware of the overall food value as well as the potential added sugar. Frequent doses of fatty burgers, chips and fried foods are not a good idea whatever your diet restraints. Wholemeal sandwiches with salad ingredients, baked potatoes, salads, grilled meat, poultry, fish and dishes with added beans or pulses, such as chilli con carne or vegetarian dishes, are all sensible options for everyday eating.

Snacks eaten out can be difficult. Digestive biscuits or crackers and cheese are the best options with coffee. Plain scones, currant buns, tea-cakes or sandwiches should be selected instead of sticky cakes, Danish pastries and Chelsea buns. Be wary of "healthy"-looking bakes like flapjacks as they often contain large quantities of added sugar.

ENTERTAINING AND DINING WITH FRIENDS

With this book entertaining certainly is not a problem. Do not feel obliged to concoct a gooey dessert for non-diabetics while the person on a restricted diet muches an apple! Everyone will feel far happier if the pudding is suitable for all the diners, particularly when it is luscious and impressive as well as being discreetly balanced.

If you are invited to a meal, then let your hosts know in advance of your diet restrictions. This is particularly appropriate if you are invited to tea, when there may be lots of cakes, but rarely a problem at more formal dinners where many people opt out of dessert these days.

ALCOHOL

Follow your doctor's recommendations. The general guidelines are to consume dry drinks rather than sweet ones (sweet wine, liqueurs, sweet sherry) in quantities less than the maximum of three units a day for men and two units a day for women. It is advisable not to drink every day (allow two or three days a week without any alcohol) and, in fact, to keep well below the maximum allowance. Alcohol has the effect of lowering the blood sugar level, so it should not be drunk on an empty stomach. Never count alcoholic drinks into your carbohydrate allowance to replace food and do not have a drink in place of food.

SUPPORT GROUPS AND ASSOCIATIONS

Lastly, your diet restrictions are not unusual and there are groups nationwide to offer advice, moral support and practical hints and tips. Find out about local groups from your clinic, doctor or dietitian. If you cannot find a local group, then join a national association.

UNITED STATES

The American Diabetes Association
National Service Center
1660 Duke Street
Alexandria, VA 22314

Juvenile Diabetes Foundation
60 Madison Avenue
New York, NY 10010

National Diabetes Information Clearing House
Box NDIC
Bethesda, MD 20205

UK

British Diabetic Association
10 Queen Anne Street
London W1M 0BD

Medic-Alert Foundation
11/13 Clifton Terrace
London N4 3JP

National Bureau for Handicapped Students
336 Brixton Road
London SW9 7AA

CANADA

The Canadian Diabetes Association

(National Office)
78 Bond Street
Toronto
Ontario M5B 2J8

AUSTRALIA

Diabetic Association of NSW
250 Pitt Street
Sydney, NSW 2000

Diabetic Association of SA
Eleanor Harrald Building
Frome Road
Adelaide, SA 5000

Diabetes Foundation (Vic)
100 Collins Street
Melbourne, Vic 3000

INDEX